BARGING IN EUROPE

How to buy and operate a barge on the
rivers and canals of continental Europe

Roger Van Dyken

Cedarbrook
Lynden, WA
ISBN 0-9651884-0-X

Illustrations by
Aminta (Van Dyken) Arrington

photos by Wendy Miller, Robert Kuehn, and the author
cover photo by Marty Haines

While every reasonable effort has been made to assure the accuracy of the information presented, this account is based on the experiences of the author. Anyone planning to cruise on Europe's waterways should conduct prudent research about the waterways, current requirements, and safety procedures. The author cannot be responsible for actions taken on account of the information presented herein.

Additional copies are available from:

Cedarbrook
131 E. Cedar Drive
Lynden, WA 98264
(360) 354-5770
FAX (360) 671-4301

Please enclose check or money order for $19.95 plus $3 shipping and handling. Washington state residents please add 7.8% sales tax ($1.79) to total.

Dedication

to my family, who not only accompanied me on the cruise, but who made my dream their own: to daughter Minti, sons Justin, Danny, and Jonathan, and especially to my quietly adventurous wife Marlene.

Acknowledgments

To Charles and Laura Rossi for taking care of our personal affairs during our absence.

To the crew at San Juan Sailing for carrying on with the business while we were gone.

To Albert Vander Veen, retired Dutch instructor of skippers, for his early advice during our cruise, his friendship, and his counsel.

To far sighted Europeans of the past five hundred years. We cruised on their visions.

And to the Europeans of today, so many of whom extended gracious hospitality and immense help to a foreign family on their waters.

Table of Contents

Introduction   6

Chapter 1 - **To Barge or Not to Barge**   9
    Why a barge?   11
    Four advantages and three disadvantages   12

Chapter 2 - **Engine Torque**   16
    Right hand or left hand shaft   16
    How to use torque to steer and stop   19

Chapter 3 - **Stopping and Turning**   21
    How to stop fast and stay straight   22
    Four turning techniques   26
    The tightest turn   30
    Ballast or Bowthruster: the surprising choice   33

Chapter 4 - **Mooring**   37
    How to avoid becoming adrift   37
    Mooring equipment   42
       Pins and land anchors   44
    Mooring against banks   45
    Mooring against city walls   47
    Mooring in marinas   49
    Anchoring techniques   53

Chapter 5 - **Locks**   59
    Types and Sizes   60
    Lock operation   61
    How to enter locks   63
    How to avoid cruising's greatest danger   65
    Customs and courtesies   76

Chapter 6 - **Meeting and Overtaking Other Boats**   84
    The "push-pull-push" effect   84
    Eight steps to avoid collision in a narrow canal   87
    Overtaking: Getting sucked in   89

Chapter 7 - **Rivers and Canals** 93
    The joys and dangers of cruising rivers 93
    The rivers of Germany 97
    Canals: self-limiting speed 102
    Canals and moorings in...
        Holland 103
        Belgium 104
        France 105
    Safely through tunnels 107

Chapter 8 - **Equipment** 111
    Packing Gland 111
    Preventive Maintenance 112
    Steering systems 116
    Choices in fenders 117
    Uses of electronic equipment 120

Chapter 9 - **Cruising Considerations** 122
    Fuel prices and strategy 122
    Mooring fees 126
    Charts 127
    Laws and Licenses 130
    Rules of the Road 132
        The Blue Flag rule 132
        Red Right Returning 134
    Person Overboard Procedures 135
    Cash, Credit Cards, and Checking Accounts 136
    Getting mail from home 138
    The best way to call home 139

Chapter 10 - **How to Buy the Right Barge** 142
    Where the best buys are 142
    Check the ballast 144
    Six items to check on the engine 147
    The survey: what to look out for 149
    How old is too old a barge? 150
    The right size--too high means you're stuck 152
    Taxes on your purchase 153
    Financing? 155

Epilogue 157

INTRODUCTION

This is the book I wished I'd read before we began our barge cruise of Europe.

Our family got off the airplane in Amsterdam. We rented a car and crisscrossed Holland inspecting barges. Then, after two weeks, we held the "great family meeting" to vote on our favorites; and we bought the barge. Happily, we made a good decision. But our choice was more good fortune than knowledgeable foresight.

We were, however, studied practitioners of sophisticated purchasing compared to our ability to handle this 120,000 pound flat bottomed steel home. Granted, we had a background in boating with my sailing business in Bellingham, Washington.

But our sailboats turned on a dime with their fin keels. This barge had no fin keel. Nothing but a flat smooth bottom that, I quickly discovered to the dread of all boaters in the vicinity, slid sideways almost as easily as forward.

Sailboats, I had told my sailing school students back home, have a lot of momentum. But nothing, I found, like our 60 ton barge. She seemed to never quit going.

Those were the biggest adjustments. A host of smaller, but extremely important differences could have landed us in real difficulty. Thankfully, they didn't.

Those experiences became accumulated lessons which we have incorporated into this compendium. You need not begin your barging as naive as we.

We experienced a year and a half of nearly continuous cruising in which we traveled over 5,000 kilometers and transited more than 900 locks. Now, it seems simple to handle our barge. And indeed it is, and has been since the first few weeks. But it didn't start out that way.

John Crowley, a fellow barger from England, remarked to me as we discussed our mutual experiences "learning to handle the barge" that it would have been so much easier had there been a practical, simple manual telling us what goes on with a barge: what the basic principles are and what to watch out for. I remember nodding my head in knowing agreement.

Out of that conversation sprouted the germ of an idea: maybe I didn't have the benefit of a practical book when I first took barge wheel in hand, but that didn't mean you who would follow in my wake should do without as well.

So this book serves as a cruising primer, covering everything from boat selection to basic principles of barge handling.

The pages that follow cover practical matters like fuel, fees, rules of the road, and licensing requirements, as well as practical basic maintenance for engines and equipment.

The book explains how to moor to a grassy canal bank so the wake and pull of a passing barge does not set you adrift, how to avoid being sucked into the hull of a passing large barge, and how to avoid breaking a leg in a lock. In short, the tricks and skills of handling your own barge.

Each country's traditions and history shape their canals, rules, costs, and procedures, from courtesies to mooring fees. I survey those factors for the primary continental cruising regions of Holland, Belgium, France and Germany.

Whether you rent or buy a barge, knowing how to handle her is critically important. Using simple layman's terms, we will see what makes a barge react the way she does. If you understand the basics, achieving finesse is much simpler. Such things as engine torque, ballast, bowthrusters, and use of fenders can either complicate life or help it, if you understand their proper role. The same is true for turning and stopping techniques. By understanding what happens when you meet or overtake a barge (or are passed by one!) you know beforehand how your barge will react.

As we visited with other experienced recreational bargers throughout Europe many told us their boat's deficiencies and the hidden shortcomings that only become apparent in the practical experiences of cruising. I note their observations as well.

Unless you have already settled on a barge, you may wish to consider a variety of craft for cruising the canals and rivers. You will find a list of the advantages and disadvantages of a barge to help you determine whether or not this is the right type of vessel for you.

Decided on a barge? Congratulations! You will need to know what to look out for and where the best buys are. The guidelines are in Chapter 10.

Although this book focuses on European barges and waterways, the principles apply to similar craft anywhere. The cardinal rules are simple. I have tried to keep explanations simple as well, illustrated by Minti's sketches.

A wonderful experience awaits you. We hope the pages that follow save you some frustration and enhance the romance of your cruise through Europe's historic web of waterways.

*   *   *   *   *   *

As I write this introduction, our family is about to board the airplane for our return to the United States at the conclusion of our 17 month family odyssey. We have cruised Holland, Belgium, France and Germany. The memories will remain forever.

This book is for those of you thinking of making your own cruising memories. You are "considering" a barge cruise through Europe. I hope that these pages help you make a wiser decision about what type of boat to cruise in and how to handle her once you are behind the wheel or handling a line in a lock.

Yet we cannot answer the ultimate question for you: Will you translate "considering" into "doing"?

There are many challenges one faces when pursuing a dream. There are a host of conventional reasons not to do it. The final decision about whether to do a barge cruise must come from deep within yourself.

Our advice: Do it. You'll never regret it.

We stop for lunch along the Canal du Rhon au Rhin

Chapter 1

TO BARGE OR NOT TO BARGE...

Why a barge? We Americans think of barges as big dirty black ocean-going things, strictly utilitarian, with no style or class. In Europe, the opposite is true. Barges have been *the* form of commercial transportation on the inland waterways since Leonardo da Vinci refined the Chinese invention of the lock, thereby facilitating inexpensive, efficient waterborne commerce and providing, in large measure, the commercial stimulus to the Renaissance.

European barges reflect history and locale. Literally hundreds of barges have been developed over the ages, reflecting local conditions and responding to technological innovations. Many were powered by sail. When the wind was adverse or nonexistent, horses along canal-side towpaths sometimes provided the power. In other cases, the power came from the bargeman and his family who either heaved on towlines or, in shallow canals, used long poles to propel the barge. Our own barge, built in 1908, has diamond rib patterned steel side decks worn smooth by thousands of wooden shoe footsteps as owner/operators propelled her by pole, arm, and leg.

With time, steam locomotives replaced animal and human power along the canals. In France, some canals still show the rusting remains of the tiny tracks where small steam engines pulled barges from lock to lock..

Along the rivers of Germany, barges were towed by large steam-driven pilot barges whose white puffing engines turned a huge gear which gripped a chain laid along the river bottom. The chain looped up from the river bed to the steam barge and back down again as the pilot boat literally pulled itself up or downstream, with several barges in tow. When an upstream string of barges met a downstream one, a delicate maneuver ensued. The huge chain needed to be unclasped to disengage one string of barges before reclasping so that the right-of-way string could pass.

Shortly after the turn of the century, some barges were equipped with their own steam engines.

The development of the diesel engine, however, revolutionized barge transportation about 1920. Diesel is still the propulsion system used today. Of course, the size and power of engines has increased dramatically.

Increased engine power permitted larger barges. Today, huge two story barges--longer than a football field--that power up and down the Rhine River at astonishing speeds personify the efficiency of horsepower and mechanics. Loaded with containerized cargo from the world's largest port, Rotterdam, they power against the current as far as Switzerland before unloading. Industries line these great watery arteries of commerce.

Yet, the veins of a pervasive smaller canal system remain. While once as essential to commerce as the circulatory system is to humans, the smaller waterways serve both as quaint reminders of a bygone commercial era and, to today's cruiser, as an important network of beautiful waterborne access routes to rural areas and villages large and small.

That is not to say that the smaller routes are forsaken by commercial barges entirely. Quite the contrary, an entire class of ubiquitous barges known as the "*peniche*" (pen-eesh') regularly ply many of these smaller waterways in the lowland countries, and in virtually all of the canals in France.

Peniches are built to the "*Napoleonic standard*". Among his many visions for a commercially united Europe--finally today being realized with the amazing momentum of the European Community (EC)--the prescient young French emperor of nearly two centuries ago set a standard for the development of waterways to replace the maze of varied sizes which reflected the fractured fiefdoms of the Middle Ages. A barge, he reasoned, should be able to load in Antwerp, Belgium and offload in Marseilles on the Mediterranean. So he specified a standard depth, width, and, most importantly, a standard sized lock. This lock, still the standard among most of the canals of France, measures five meters wide by 45 meters long. Accordingly, the peniche class barges are five meters wide by 38.5 meters long (to allow room for the lock gates to open). They shoehorn into the locks with bare centimeters to spare.

The peniches are the equivalent of the American small family farm, usually owner-operated, often with wife and small children aboard. And like the family farm, it struggles against intense competition. Even though each peniche transports the equivalent of ten 30 ton trucks with the same size motor as one truck, these venerable craft are threatened by larger barges and by railroads. Many peniches are now converted to liveaboard homes and cruise ships under government sponsored buyout programs whose purpose is to reduce the number of peniches so the remainder may survive. We regularly offer a toast to their survival.

As a consequence, there are two sources of barges for the prospective barge cruiser: converted or retired peniches and the older, more stylish lowland barges from the turn of the century. The peniches are a bit boxy but have immense amounts of room. Just calculate for a moment. Even without the upper level wheelhouse or sun deck, each peniche can provide over 2,000 square feet of interior living space, a very favorable comparison to the size of many American homes! Most excess peniches are converted to luxury hotel barges that cruise the European waterways, catering to tourists for $2,000 to $3,000 per person per week, all services provided. Other peniches serve as permanent homes for sky-high-rent Parisians whose converted barges line the banks of the Seine River within Paris and for miles in either direction.

The older, smaller barges of the lowland countries, particularly the Netherlands, provide the most accessible, affordable, and easy to handle barges for the cruising family. After a quick glance at the boat, a knowledgeable Dutchman will be able to tell approximately when she was built and the style she represents, not unlike Americans picking out a '55 Chevy or a '57 Thunderbird. The big breasted bows of the "*Tjalks*" (chall'-iks) contrast with the finer entry of the "*Klipper Aaks*" ("*Aak*" is Dutch for "barge") or the regional lines of the "*Ijssel Aak*" (which was developed along the river *Ijssel*), to mention just a few of the myriad of types and styles.

A basic question needs answering, however. Should you choose a barge or another type of boat? It's a good question. After all, barges are "different" to us Americans. What are their advantages and disadvantages? You are reading this book, so you probably have some "*water in your blood*", as the Dutch like to say. Maybe you simply possess the most essential ingredient: the ability to follow your dream. Or perhaps you have a background in boating that provides a "comfort zone" as you approach the idea of cruising the canals and rivers of Europe.

If you are a sailor, you naturally will want to investigate using a sailboat through the inland waterways. I certainly did. After much resistance to the idea of anything but a sailboat, time and study finally convinced me of the wisdom of Christian Uehr, a German sailing friend. "*If you plan to be in the Baltic, the North Sea, the Atlantic, or the Mediterranean, come in a sailboat*", he said. "*But if you plan to do the rivers and canals, get a boat designed for the purpose. Get a barge.*" His proved to be excellent advice.

If you are set on a sailboat, however, or perhaps are sailing to Europe via the Atlantic, or plan to spend most of your time sailing the seas and little time in the canals, it is possible. These are some realities to consider, however.

Space: few sailboats can match the spaciousness of the barge, and if they can, they don't belong on a canal. Fact of life.

Draft: barges usually have about a one meter (39 inches) draft. Though the Napoleonic standard stipulates a two meter depth, many French canals are 1.2 to 1.4 meters deep, meaning many sailboats will go aground regularly as they maneuver near canal banks around passing barges, or as they moor, or enter locks. Excess draft severely constrains choice of canals.

Sailing in canals: It's impossible on all but a few large canals and rivers, and those are almost exclusively in Holland. So the mast and boom are unstepped and strapped to the deck, which makes an impediment to other boats as well as to yourself as you maneuver in a lock in the wash of a 100+ horsepower barge.

But what of a conventional powerboat, you ask? Definitely possible and, for many, practical. Before making a decision, however, consider these **advantages** of the barge:

1. Barges are **less expensive**, either to charter or to buy. They provide more room for less money. While prices will vary considerably based on the size and interior of the barge and the equipment she carries, in our experience--and as of this writing--she will probably cost about 1/4 as much to buy as a comparably sized conventional powerboat, on a square foot basis. For any family on a budget, that is a factor to consider.

2. **Moorage costs are often less** for barges. Barges are bigger and moorage is assessed by the meter. How can moorage be less? The answer lies in the fact that old converted barges are neither fish nor fowl. They are normally too large for marinas and not really suitable for mooring in the middle of the huge commercial barges. So where do you moor? Pretty much wherever you want to--along a canal bank, by a city wall, in lakes, or sometimes, by permission, next to a commercial barge.

There are exceptions, of course. Many Dutch towns will charge you for staying in their city limits, especially in Friesland. In 1993, they charged about 1 guilder (around 65 cents) per meter length, which is still cheaper than marinas.

3. Barges are **stronger**. These iron or steel craft are older, but they are solidly made and can take a lot of abuse.

I remember well docking on the Ijssel River at Kampen in northeast Holland (actually Holland is a province of the Netherlands. But nearly everyone refers to the Netherlands as Holland, so I will too.) I had to maneuver our 70 foot, 60 ton barge into about a 90 foot space between two boats at the mooring on the wall, against the current. I had about two weeks experience at the time. Worse, the mooring was to starboard (see chapter 6), and the torque as I hit reverse forced the bow into the mooring. I bumped the mooring wall. I was embarrassed, which was evidently noted by the skipper of the Grand Banks cruiser moored just ahead of me. Though I didn't know it at the time, this gray-haired gentleman lounging on his after deck was Anne Wever, maker of the highly respected line of Trintella sailboats. As I tightened the bow line, Mr. Wever smiled and said in classic Dutch brogue, *"Not to worry, son. No damage. This boat was around long before you were and she will still be sailing long after you are gone."*

Our barge is nearly ninety years old. Initially, I was concerned at her age, worried about rust, electrolytic corrosion, galvanic corrosion, and all the related concerns to those of us who sail in salt waters. But the world is different for these fresh water boats. As Klaus, the assistant foreman at a competent Dutch yard remarked to me, *"The rust is mostly all out"*. I smiled, thinking he was joking. But he was serious. Many lifelong barge skippers have underscored the point to me. Old steel is good steel, as long as the minimum thickness (4 mm) is still there. And iron, prevalent on boats built before 1900, is even better. Of course, make sure the boat is solid; just because she is old and floating doesn't necessarily mean she is sound.

A **good** old barge is a proven barge. She can be trusted, despite what us "newness" oriented Americans tend to think by reflex.

4. You **don't bounce so much** on a barge. You can moor fairly comfortably along the Seine in Paris for example, while the turbulence from constant tour boats drives conventional powerboats to the protection of

expensive marinas. That stability is also valuable as you maneuver in the wash of big barges in locks. Power boaters tell disturbing tales of their experiences bouncing off lock walls.

Barges also have **disadvantages**. Consider these:

1. **Old equipment**. Not always true, but often old barges are floating antiques. Old equipment may be fine, but it also may need more repairs while underway.

When we bought our barge, she had a wonderful antique engine aboard—1922 single cylinder model. On our first cruise I had a frantic report from one of the children that *"water is all over the engine room"* Quickly diving below, I gazed at the giant exterior flywheel as it dipped into an overfull bilge, picked up water and slung it in a 360 degree arc on the overhead, the bulkheads—everywhere. The camel skin flange—you read right, camel skin!—on the ancient water pump had broken, so the trusty pump was leaking water into the boat with each stroke, as well as pushing it into the engine. The bilge water level had risen to the bottom of the flywheel. I turned on the bilge pump and discovered to my dismay that the bilge pump water and the engine cooling water were both routed to the same pipe. There was so much pressure from the cooling water that the bilge pump couldn't get its water out! In other words, the boat was filling with water and the bilge pump could not do its job with the engine running. And since it took 15 minutes to start that wonderful antique engine, turning the engine off momentarily to keep ahead of the rising water was out of the question. Although ingenuity born of necessity managed a temporary solution, we soon discovered camel skin was in short supply and I realized this beautiful old 20 horsepower single cylinder Kromhout showpiece may have to be retired. We replaced her with a 165 horsepower Dutch DAF diesel engine and cruised 3,000 miles with reliable modern power. Old equipment is not necessarily bad, but bears close examination.

2. Barges are **not as maneuverable**. What you gain in stability you lose in maneuverability. A conventional powerboat responds more quickly to get in and out of tight places. Yet, I stand in awe of the grace with which the professional barge skippers handle their behemoths like a dinghy; but it takes years of practice to become that good.

3. **Slower resale**. There are far more conventional powerboats than converted barges. That means a much larger market for a conventional craft upon resale. True, they are not manufacturing turn of the century barges anymore and many project their value will continue to increase, but that is speculation. Powerboat resale is more of a sure thing.

You may be surprised by one non-factor: speed. Of course, conventional powerboats can go faster than barges, if that is your aim. But they seldom have the opportunity to use their speed. Canals have strict speed limits. Besides, it is common sense to avoid making big wakes that erode canal banks and disturb fellow boaters. As a practical matter, boats of all sizes on small and medium sized canals all cruise at more or less the same speed.

So, what is the best boat for you—sail, powerboat, or barge? In the final analysis, only you can answer that question. We boaters are emotional in our nautical choices. But if you follow practical guidelines in your selection, you will be as happy several weeks into your cruise as you are when you begin it.

Although this book is written primarily for handling barges, the sections on waterways, rules of the road, locks, and guidelines for each country apply to sail and powerboats as well. Plus, with some knowledge of barge handling, you will be better prepared to maneuver side by side with a large commercial barge in that tight lock with only happy results, no matter what craft you are piloting.

Chapter 2

HARNESSING ENGINE TORQUE

Engine torque is simply the way the propeller moves the stern either to the starboard (right) or port (left). Put the transmission in forward and the stern will move one way; put it in reverse and it will move the opposite. Determining how it does this is quite straightforward. However, we then need to visualize it, and memorize which way it goes in either forward or reverse. When you master torque you will deftly maneuver your barge like an old pro.

Torque is an intimidating word. It somehow sounds technical and macho all at once. It was one of those pre-turbo words dropped by high school seniors when talking to freshmen that made them nod in astonishment. And all it really means for us boaters is slipping sideways.

Here's how it works. The engine turns the prop and the prop rotates in a particular direction. The prop wants to make the boat go sideways in the direction that it rotates. That's all. So if the prop turns to the right, the boat will want to move to the right. If the prop turns to the left, the boat will want to move to the left.

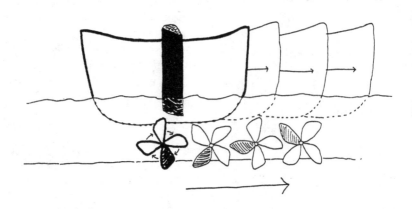

Picture it in your mind. In your mental picture, take the propeller off the boat and put the wheel from your car there instead. Now take most of the water out of the canal, so your boat is resting on that car tire and the car tire is on the bottom of the canal. Now put the engine in gear and watch your wheel rotate. Which way is it turning? Is it turning to the right? If so, the back of your boat will get a nice ride toward the right bank, correct? Now, put the transmission in reverse. Your wheel turns the opposite way. Now the boat is heading for the left bank. Good. Well, now put the propeller back on because that's the same action the propeller makes. It just moves through the water and makes your boat "swim" sideways in the same direction the imaginary car tire carried the boat.

Please note that the propeller is on the stern of the boat. Only the back of the boat is being carried sideways to the shore with the engine in gear. In fact, if you were to look closely, you would see the barge act a little like a sideways teeter totter and pivot a bit on its center so that the front of the boat (the bow) actually heads slightly in the opposite direction.

To illustrate, take a pencil and lay it on the table. With your finger, lightly flick the eraser end sideways. What happens to the pointy end? It goes a bit in the opposite direction, right? So when your stern goes to starboard, your bow will go slightly to port; and vice versa.

First, let's determine whether your particular boat has a left or a right hand turning prop. Here's what we do: Put the transmission into forward. Now, stand aft of the engine and, facing forward, (toward the bow of the boat) look at the propeller shaft. Is it turning to the right (clockwise, to starboard)? If so, you have a **right hand** turning propeller. The stern will walk to the right, or starboard, when in forward. If, however, you see the propeller shaft turning to the left or counterclockwise, the stern will walk to the left, or port, when in forward.

Now, and very important, whichever way she walks in forward, she will go the opposite direction in reverse. For example, if the stern slips to starboard when accelerating in forward, the stern will move to port when accelerating in reverse.

You are now ready for the final two steps.

Step one: **visualize**. Paint a picture in your mind that shows the prop turning in its direction in forward and the stern responding by shifting sideways in that same direction. Now paint a second picture in reverse gear. See the prop turn the opposite direction? And see the stern go in that direction? Now make that picture an action video. See yourself with your hand on the gearshift, as you mentally push the gearshift forward.

As the prop turns, look out at the water and see the prop torque moving you sideways. Slip the engine into reverse and see the opposite occurring. Now run and rerun the video numerous times until the images are firmly in your mind.

Step two: **Memorize**. If your prop is right hand turning, memorize **forward-starboard**; **reverse-port**. If your prop is left hand turning, memorize the opposite.

I emphasize visualizing and memorizing torque effect because this concept is basic. It is foundational. Every day you cruise it will affect you. If you understand it, it will make your handling so much easier. On the other hand, if you are sometimes confused about what torque is going to do to you in forward or reverse, you will never master your barge.

You need be able to visualize that video automatically and instantly. Here's why. At some time you will find yourself in a tight situation, one you had not planned on. A boat will pull out in front of you, or you will need to get near enough to the wall of a lock to moor, or you need to get out of the way of something important.

Let me drive the point home. Imagine the worst—you enter a lock and, when the barge is nearly stopped but still moving, a loved one near the stern reaches to put a mooring line on the bollard in the port lock wall. You are a few feet from the lock wall. Your dear one reaches, slips, and falls in the water. Now what do you do? You need to know without thinking that if your shaft is right hand turning (as most of them are), accelerating in reverse will move the stern to port. If that's the action you take to stop the boat immediately, you will bring the boat into the wall, squeezing your crew between the hull and the side of the lock. In addition, the prop wash will tend to suck that person into the prop. Knowing these things instantly, you won't make that mistake. Instead, you will turn the wheel hard to port, so the stern swings away from your crew to avoid crushing them; that will also push the bow into the lock wall, helping to slow the boat; and you will not engage reverse until your crew is well clear of the boat. Visualizing instantly will make the difference between a laughable accident and potential tragedy.

Now that you have the foundation firmly established in your mind, we can construct some of the finer points of torque. One has to do with ballast. The more ballast, or weight, the lower in the water the boat sits. The lower in the water, the more resistance to sideways movement.

Realize that you have a flat bottomed boat, one that slides sideways almost as easily as it slides forward, especially if your barge basically sits on top of the water. The more it "sinks" into the water, the more the sides of the hull push against the water like a bulldozer anytime the boat wants to move sideways. So the greater the ballast, the less the effect of torque. Conversely, if there is little ballast aboard to lower the hull into the water, engine torque will be very strong. A strong argument for a well-ballasted barge.

Engine speed also affects engine torque. This one is easy to follow: the faster the prop speed, the greater the torque. So if yours is a right hand turning shaft and the barge is moored to port, a brief engine burst while in forward gear will move your stern away from the dock. Conversely, when docking, a brief burst in reverse will move your stern nicely into the dock as you stop. Very sharp maneuver, with a little practice.

Consider also the effect of torque while just tootling down a straight canal. With constant engine speed and running straight, will you still have torque? Yes, you will. But not as much. The principle here is this: the slower the boat speed compared to engine speed, the greater the effect of engine torque. The faster the boat speed, the less effect.

But there still is a slight torque when moving down the canal at cruising speed. While cruising, let go of the steering wheel and see where the barge heads. The barge will tend to head slightly off to one side or the other. That's because of engine torque. Once again, a right hand turning prop will always want to swing the stern to starboard, pushing the bow to port. To counteract that tendency, keep the steering wheel pressed slightly to starboard.

The greater the ballast, of course, the less the tendency to head to port and the less you need to hold the steering wheel to starboard. Incidentally, a convenient way to counteract torque while underway is to rest a stockinged foot on a spoke of the wheel. Even on a mechanical steering system, light foot pressure is usually sufficient to compensate for torque and keep the barge headed straight down the canal.

Torque also affects stopping. When using reverse gear to stop--and given the weight of barges, you need reverse to overcome that momentum--your stern will move sideways in response to reverse torque. In addition, as the barge gradually slows, the stern will slip sideways more because, remember, the slower your boat speed compared to engine speed, the greater the torque effect. As the barge stops, your stern will really be swinging, and you may end up somewhat crosswise in the canal, at least not as nice and straight as you would like. As you slow or stop before entering a lock, being other than straight is disconcerting.

What do you do to avoid ending up crosswise in a canal after you engage reverse to slow or stop? Simple. Turn the wheel as you stop. As you slip the transmission into reverse, give the wheel a turn. As you accelerate in reverse, turn the wheel more. Experiment a little. With a bit of practice you will sense the right amount of wheel to counteract the torque. Your barge will end up stopped straight.

Let's move from stopping straight to turning. Using torque to your advantage can make your turns surprisingly crisp, especially considering you are piloting a flat bottomed craft. By using the natural tendency of the stern to swing one way or the other with torque, we can make a much tighter turn. Not only does the rudder kick the stern to the side, but so does the torque of the propeller, giving two forces, working in concert to accentuate our turning motion. Think about this maneuver. Visualize it. If the picture is not crystal clear, put the car tire back onto the drive shaft. Now, in addition, see how the water pushes against the side of the rudder, forcing the stern sideways also. Got it? Good!

When you clearly understand and can instantly visualize the prop direction and its sideways effect on the barge, it will be much easier to turn, stop, moor, and depart. You are harnessing torque to your advantage and are well on your way to mastering the art.

We will look more closely at stopping and turning techniques in the next chapter.

Chapter 3

STOPPING AND TURNING

This chapter will cover techniques for stopping and turning the barge in a variety of situations. We will also look at the effects on turning of ballast and bowthrusters.

STOPPING

Ahead you see one of the many locks you will enter as you alternately climb and descend through the rolling Burgundy region of France. You ease the throttle into neutral early on, and coast on your craft's considerable momentum, there being very little to slow the barge. The tarred bottom has a slippery thin covering of feathery algae but no barnacle-like growths to make you lug through the water. The ponderous velocity from your vessel's considerable weight is not easily diminished.

As the barge slowly approaches the closed black steel gates of the lock, you note for the umpteenth time that the width of the lock is 5 meters (about 16 feet), precisely the Napoleonic standard. Your barge is just a bit narrower than 5 meters so you need to enter the gates straight.

The gates crack open as you approach, indicating the automatic system on this stretch of canal is working properly. The electric eye on the lock you exited a few kilometers back apparently sent its electronic signal to this lock, preparing it for your arrival. The timing is just about right, you sense: your momentum should bring you to the gates of the lock a few seconds after they are fully open and ready for you to enter.

As the lock gates crank open a bit more you peer between them to see--black. To your shock, it's not the black of the gates on the far side of the lock, it's the black of a hull. A peniche--built to fill the lock to its absolute maximum capacity--is about to leave the lock, headed straight for you.

Mentally, you quickly shift gears. Now, instead of coasting smoothly through the lock gates, you need to come to a very prompt halt. Not only that, you need to allow the barge to pass beside you, and after it has gone, to maneuver your barge back into the center of the canal positioned to enter the gates straight.

There are subsequent chapters that introduce you to meeting barges and maneuvering. But right now your mind is concentrating on step number one: how to get the barge stopped quickly.

Well, that's quite simple, you think, and it really is. You slip the transmission into reverse and accelerate gradually but firmly, as the 3 foot diameter bronze propeller churns against your craft's momentum, gradually slowing you to a stop.

Then you notice something disconcerting. Your barge is stopping all right, but the stern is swinging to port and the bow to starboard. What can you do? You have to keep the boat solidly in reverse to stop, so you can't let up.

The lock gates are now almost fully open and the awesome eight foot high black bow will emerge in a few seconds. With a helpless feeling you slide more and more sideways until your barge blocks the entire canal, your bow near the right bank, your stern on the left.

Then, a clunk! bang! comes from the back of the boat. Instantly, you realize the propeller has hit chunks of cement set to protect the vulnerable base of the canal banks and you hope fervently that the prop still has all its blades. Your peripheral vision catches that huge black hulk heading out of the lock, its bow so high you are sure its skipper cannot possibly see you--his view obscured by the lock walls on either side and the unloaded bow sitting high in the water. Frantically, you reach for this book, wishing you had read this section and hoping against hope it will quickly tell you exactly what to do now!

When dealing with masses of moving metal, prevention is definitely the preferred cure. So let's go back to the beginning and see how we could have avoided this predicament; back to the moment we discovered that the lock held a barge and that you needed to stop very quickly.

How could we have prevented that cross-canal juxtaposition? In two ways: by "anticipative steering" and, if necessary, forward thrusting.

As soon as you put it in reverse, you remembered **reverse port**. The torque from the right hand turning prop (assuming it is--the opposite applies if it is a left hand turning prop) nudges the stern to starboard in forward, and to port in reverse. Having read chapter two on torque thoroughly, you know that the barge's torque in this stopping situation will be accentuated both by high engine RPMs and by ever decreasing boat speed through the water. Since you are stopping suddenly, the engine RPMs are definitely up and, as the reverse gear takes effect, the barge is also definitely slowing. As a consequence, torque effect is at its maximum, which is why your stern in the nightmare above behaved in a manner you weren't used to.

With these factors in mind, you will prevent potential disaster as you accelerate in reverse, by simply turning the wheel sharply to port (stop and visualize this now) so the rudder pushes your stern to starboard. This counteracts the push-to-port effect of propeller torque while in reverse. As the boat slows, less water will be streaming by the rudder, and its effect will be significantly diminished. Plus, such heavy thrashing of the water by the prop, just in front of the rudder will disturb even more the water flowing by the rudder, further reducing its effectiveness. The trick therefore, as I alluded to in Chapter 2, is to put the rudder over early, as early as possible, while it still has maximum effect. If you have the presence of mind, swing the wheel to port just before you hit reverse.

With practice, by synchronizing rudder and reverse properly for the nuances of your craft, you will be able to stop precisely straight, to the amazement and respect of the oncoming professional bargeman, who knows exactly the forces you are dealing with.

But let's say that you didn't swing the rudder quite on time and despite your best efforts, your stern is slowly but definitely heading to port, right toward the bank and those pieces of concrete. Don't panic. All is not lost. In fact, you can use that slight setting of your stern to port (keep up the mental picture here) to get out of the way of the barge which will be coming toward you in a minute or so. Here's how.

Watch your stern now. Before it gets too close to the bank, and definitely before you are in danger of hitting rocks with your prop, pop the gearshift into neutral, pause momentarily and shift it into forward, then give it a strong spurt. Remember you already have the wheel hard to port. So the rudder is in the ideal position for this forward thrust. The prop will suddenly push massive amounts of water--if only for a moment--against the rudder, pushing the stern to starboard. The burst in forward starts a tight turn to port. See how that straightens the barge in the canal? Beautiful!

Now slip the gearshift back to neutral, pause, and return to accelerated reverse. Repeat this little reverse-forward maneuver several times if necessary as you nurse the barge to a straight stop at the side of the canal. The peniche just now leaving the lock can pass by, leaving your metal unmolested. Nicely done!

You have used the principle of torque to your advantage. You have visualized immediately the **reverse port** stern direction caused by torque, realized that it would be accentuated by high engine RPMs and by ever slower boat speed. Your steering anticipated the need to counteract the torque. Then you used the rudder and **forward starboard** torque in combination to straighten out the barge and position her properly for the oncoming traffic.

Now that we saved our prop, our pride, and possibly our hull at the lock, there is one other factor we have not yet addressed that will affect your ability to stop and stay in position. It may sneak up on you. You can't see it and, enclosed in a pilothouse, you can't feel it. But with the amount of exposed superstructure a barge has, believe me, wind is a most significant factor in barge handling. I have seen unloaded commercial barges with very little hull in the water and a seemingly towering black hulk exposed to the wind, go down river at an angle, their bows canted into the wind like an airplane trying to land in a cross wind. And, of course, the slower the speed of the barge, the more significant the wind effect. When stopped, the barge is totally at the mercy of the wind.

If you are in a *narrow* canal waiting for a bridge to raise or a lock to open, stop to leeward (the direction the wind is blowing *toward*). The wind will blow the barge into the bank, out of the way of the oncoming vessel where you can relax and wait until it passes. Then pole off, first the bow and then the stern, making sure the stern is well clear, repeat, well clear of the bank and of any concrete or rocks lying in wait to bend your prop.

On the other hand, if you are waiting in a larger canal, move to the windward side where there is enough room to occasionally maneuver back to windward. Larger canals often have more gently sloping sides and it could well be difficult to unground the barge from the leeward bank against a strong breeze.

Many locks and bridges in larger canals have a series of clustered wooden dolphins (usually a tight group of large poles driven into the canal bottom and bound together by cables at the top) usually on the starboard side of each approach, but sometimes on both sides of each approach. Tie onto a windward dolphin if possible. The dolphins are frequently spaced for the large commercial barges and may be too far apart for you to tie to two dolphins. In that case, secure a line from the dolphin to your forward boat bollards. The wind will gradually push the stern sideways but remember the stern is very maneuverable with the very large rudders that barges have. Slowly engage the transmission forward and turn the wheel as desired to keep the barge straight.

One word of caution here as you moor. Until the side of the bow rests firmly against the dolphin, come up very, very slowly with the engine. Novices will come up too fast and the securing line will suddenly come taut, causing the side of the bow to crash into the dolphin. The crew will look back at their skipper with a withering look that spoils the atmosphere of the candlelit dinner you had planned. So, after the crew has the line between the dolphin and the boat bollard secured, move the boat extremely slowly until the line gradually comes taut and the boat is snugged up against the dolphin (or wall, or dock; this principle applies in a variety of situations). Then you may add power to your heart's content.

Back to wind forces. When the wind is from aft (directly behind you), make sure to slow down very, very early when approaching an opening bridge or lock. Otherwise the wind will boost your momentum and only strong reverse on the engine will slow the barge. That brings on reverse torque and if your stern shifts to port with a strong wind from behind...

Wind will also force you to alter mooring tactics. If mooring downwind (to leeward) in a crosswind, bring the barge to a stop a few feet off the dock and let the breeze blow you gently into the dock. On the other hand, when mooring to windward in a strong cross wind, nose the bow in and have your crew secure it. Once the bow is well secured, you can easily bring in the stern with propeller and rudder. Just remember the precautions discussed above about slowly snugging up against your mooring before accelerating the engine.

Now you know the principles to make you a highly competent stopper. Stopping a barge requires a bit more finesse than stepping on the brake to stop your car for a traffic jam. After all, your barge has no brakes. But it's a lot more fun stopping your barge on a canal in France or Holland than stopping your car on the LA freeway for the hundredth time in a morning.

TURNING

You will be surprised how often you will want to make a U-turn in a canal. Maybe it's after a day cruise, or after visiting a city. Perhaps you just realized you left your spouse waiting on the dock. Or, like me, you lose your favorite cap to a strong wind and want to go back for it. But most frequently, you will do U-turns while preparing to moor in a harbor.

Technique: **Stop before you make a U-turn.**

As you prepare to make the U-turn, remember one critical consideration: **STOP** first--totally, dead stopped. Only if there is a long, and I mean loooong, straight stretch of water out in front can you get by without stopping before initiating the turn. For the reason, let's go back to the basics.

With its flat bottom, a barge slides sideways nearly as easily as forward. As a result, when turning you may well find yourself, with the barge's considerable momentum, sliding sideways. The barge will still be going in her original direction, but broadside.

Attempting a U-turn while traveling even at a very slow speed can mean trouble.

> We entered the small barge harbor at Dordrecht, the Netherlands. Because the harbor was so narrow, we had to maneuver forward and aft several times as we attempted to complete a U-turn before mooring. When I began the turn, I had a bit--only a little bit--of boat speed. And as I alternated between forward and reverse trying to complete the turn, I still had only a little bit of boat speed. Unfortunately it was in the same direction as I started--which was now sideways. I was running out of room in the tiny harbor.
>
> Slowly, inexorably, our barge was slipping sideways toward a barge moored at the far end of the little harbor. Only by a quick prayer, a lot of sweat, and one more wrinkle in my forehead did I manage to complete my turn in time. What a relief to be able to turn my stern toward the barge I was about to hit broadside and power away from her. The helplessness I had felt while sliding sideways was nearly overwhelming. I could maneuver forward or aft, but when sliding sideways there was no control available to halt that sickening slide. However, had I **stopped** first, I would have had no problem.

Technique: **accelerate out of a turn.**

There is a way to stop that sideways drift in an unwanted direction. But you can only use this control if there is enough room forward. The principle is this: forward momentum can overcome sideways momentum. In other words, if the barge is sliding helplessly sideways, put her in forward and accelerate sharply. The new momentum created by the thrust of the propeller will overcome the broadside momentum and put the barge in a new forward direction. This is dependent, of course, on having plenty of open water in the direction of your new momentum.

For example, imagine a canal intersection. A sharp right hand turn with the transmission in neutral would cause the barge to skid around the corner. You might even hit the far bank. By adding power well into the turn, however, one can overcome sideways momentum with a new, more powerful forward momentum. Hence the advice: *go slow into a turn, power out of it.*

Remember when your car driving instructor taught you not to hit the brakes in the middle of a turn but to push gently on the gas pedal instead? The same principle holds true for handling a barge.

There are limitations to this principle, however. Putting the gearshift in forward is not an instant and complete cure to sideways drift. There are two competing momentums at work here. The second must be powerful enough to overcome the first. Sometimes that requires a judgment call as to which competing momentum--sideways or forward--will win out.

> Our barge nosed through the beautifully serpentine River Leie just south of Ghent, Belgium. The scenery has inspired authors and artists, a fact we could fully appreciate as we pushed through the morning mists which hovered above manicured lawns and classic homes adorning the river banks. Distracted by the mystic beauty, I failed to pay close enough attention to the chart. As we neared Ghent the River Leie appeared to swing 90 degrees to the left. This was not unusual; we had been powering our way out of hairpin turns all morning. Then suddenly, I noticed the river simultaneously veered 90 degrees to the right. This was not a curve, it was a "Y". Which way to go?
>
> The left was the broader stream so I maintained that heading while I searched frantically to find myself on

the chart. Oh no! According to the chart, the branch to the left where I was headed petered out to nothing and I would have to back out! Now, however, I was so committed to the left hand part of the "Y", I wondered if I could still switch to starboard.

I swung the wheel sharply to the right.

Keep in mind our speed was pretty normal, a little slower than usual, perhaps, given the curving beauty of this charming little river, but I certainly had plenty of momentum. As I started my turn, I was shifting the barge's momentum from the left and toward the right--well, actually smack between the left and the right, directly toward the base of the "Y", where one would hope to find a nice soft bank to slide sideways into should I not successfully power out of this turn. No such luck! A neat row of small boats with eminently crunchable fiberglass hulls lined the bank at the base of the "Y". They would be no match for 120,000 pounds of steel hull sideswiping them in full thrust as I tried to power out of the turn.

I was confronted with a college physics question that demanded an instant answer: If I turned the barge sharply to the right and hit full power forward, would propeller thrust give me enough new forward momentum to overcome my original momentum (which was now sideways, toward that line of fragile boats at the base of the "Y")? Or would the original momentum win out, so that as I skidded around the turn at full power, I would broadside into those tiny vulnerable craft? No time for complex calculations. Each moment was taking me closer to those boats. I had to make a decision.

Frankly, I don't know if I made the correct one. Upon reflection, I doubt it. My choice was conservative. If I tried to power out of the turn, I thought I probably would be able to make it. But if I didn't make it, I would not only sideswipe those boats, but with full power, the damage would be--well, I didn't want to imagine it. The mental picture was enough for me to choose the less risky option.

I straightened the barge as much and as quickly as I could, back to a straight course, which put my bow headed directly at those little boats at the bank. At the same time I eased the transmission into reverse and then accelerated sharply. The engine roared. Smoke billowed from the exhaust.

My strategy was simple: try to stop before crunching the little boats. As you realize fully, especially after reading the above section on stopping, it takes a while to stop a barge. And with your knowledge of engine torque, you can predict what would happen. Though I was heading almost straight for the boats, the torque from my thrashing prop moved the stern to port (our barge "Vertrouwen" has a right hand turning prop, as do most barges). As she slowed, the effect of torque was more pronounced, moving the stern more definitely to port. We slowed, though not quickly enough, and our stern torqued around so that we were nearly stopped as we were broadside to the boats. We watched helplessly as our last little bit of momentum slowly drifted us into the boats. In fact, toward the end of the maneuver, I was able to play with engine torque and rudder so that we were exactly sideways to the little boats, softening our impact by touching all of them simultaneously rather than having one boat take the entire impact. I was able to minimize our momentum enough to avoid damage.

We were stopped. No harm done. My conservative calculations worked, kind of. Yet, a more experienced skipper may have avoided the situation entirely, first by religiously following the chart; second, possibly by powering out of the turn; or third, by turning the wheel hard to port at the beginning of the maneuver, which would have kept the barge straight and stopped short of the boats.

Can you visualize the competing momentums? Good. That will help you avoid my mistakes.

Now let's look at **torqueing your turns**.

But first, review what happens with torque--the force that moves the barge sideways in response to the propeller's rotation. Recall that the stern will "walk" in the direction the propeller turns. The more common right hand turning prop moves the stern to the right (starboard) in forward. Conversely, a left hand turning prop will kick the stern to left (port) in forward.

Let's assume that you have a right hand turning prop, so torque shoves the stern *to starboard in forward, right?* Do you have that visualized? Good. Here's how we apply it.

Technique: the tightest turn is in the direction opposite the torque.

With torque to starboard, the sharpest turn is to port. You can see it, can't you? Both the rudder and the torque move the stern to starboard, pivoting the barge neatly toward your new direction to port.

Given that bit of theory, here is how to apply it to a U-turn on the canals. If there is a w-i-d-e area in which to make the U-turn, do so by turning to port. Having stopped (unless there is a long straight stretch of canal before you), turn the wheel hard to port, fine tune forward thrust for maximum torque and execute a nice tight U-turn (providing wind is not a problem), heading off in the direction from which you came. Easy enough.

However, if the canal is too narrow to complete the U-turn without stopping and backing up--and you will become a good judge of that after a few U-turns--you must turn the opposite direction. Instead of making the turn to port, make the turn hard to starboard. Why? Because when you hit reverse and back up, torque will now be on your side. With a right hand turning prop, in forward the torque is to starboard, in reverse it is to port. The rudder and torque now take turns helping execute the turn. The rudder, hard to starboard, (visualize!) moves the stern to port when the propeller is in forward. And reverse torque also moves the stern to port when the propeller is in reverse. Regardless of whether the propeller is in forward or reverse, the stern is being swung to port and the bow to starboard, completing your pirouette in mid-canal.

Let's try to illustrate by mixing a new principle into the ingredients at work here. Remember the discussion of momentum and how once the barge heads in a particular direction, she is hard to stop, whether that be forward or sideways? Here is how one can use momentum to advantage.

In a turning situation, the principle of momentum translates into this: get the bow to move in the direction you want and it will likely keep going that way. Now quickly back to your right hand turn. When you kicked the wheel over to the right and began the U-turn, you started the bow moving from left to right. (Stop and picture this). Unable to complete the turn before the grassy canal bank gets in the way, you switch gears gently from forward to reverse, and accelerate in reverse. Torque is now to port and here is the important part. That reverse torque to port keeps the barge turning! It keeps the stern moving to port and keeps the bow swinging to starboard.

The rudder starts the turn by swinging the stern to port. Then, reverse torque maintains the stern's momentum to port. In fact, if the turn is extremely tight, and we have made U-turns in canals with only a two to three foot clearance bank to bank, you may be able to simply leave the rudder hard to starboard while alternating forward and reverse. Put the rudder hard over and turn with only the transmission handle! Forward pushes the stern to port because of the propeller's wash against the rudder and reverse also moves the stern to port, thanks to torque.

The result can leave spectators in awed wonderment. With a canal so narrow it is barely wider than the length of your barge, you crank the rudder hard to starboard, spinning gently on your axis as you effortlessly alternate tiny bursts of power in forward and reverse. Beautiful!

Now that you have mastered stops and turns by applying torque, thrust, and momentum in precise practiced proportions, let me add an additional factor. I hinted at it earlier and you may have guessed. Wind. Strong wind.

Brisk breezes are prevalent on hot summer afternoons in the lowland countries, especially the Netherlands. It is no accident that expert sailors and sailboarders hail from Holland. They get lots of practice. The same wind that drives a sailboat or sailboard will try to do the same with your barge. The only difference is that your sail is steel, doesn't develop lift, and is attached to a far heavier boat. So it tends to move the barge sideways instead of forward.

As indicated elsewhere, the less ballast the barge has, the more susceptible it will be to wind forces; another argument for a properly ballasted boat. Yet even the best ballasted boat will have to contend with wind as it turns or stops, just to less of a degree than the sister ship sitting high on the water with lots of hull and cabin up there trying to block the wind. In fact, even a properly ballasted boat will have a very difficult time completing a U-turn with a strong following wind. A poorly ballasted barge will find it virtually impossible. The barge just doesn't seem to be able to turn her bow into the wind. Try it a few times. It doesn't work. The barge just won't turn up into that stiff breeze. But you need to turn around. What to do?

Technique: spin around your anchor

Drop the anchor in mid-channel and let the barge swing around it. The anchor does not need to hold very fast for this to work. Raise the anchor as you begin to move into the wind. This method is commonly used on older commercial barges. Or else use the following.

Technique: put the bow into the bank

The concept here is quite simple. Instead of trying to turn while floating free on the water, secure the bow of the boat and turn around it, so to speak.

Get as close to 90 degrees to the bank as you can. Then gently nudge the bow into a soft, grassy canal bank. Put the rudder hard over and power up strongly, both to keep the bow wedged firmly into the bank, and to get the stern moving sideways in the direction of your turn. The pressure of the bow pressing into the bank helps overcome the effect of wind against the hull and allows the turn despite the wind.

What if there is no grassy bank? Perhaps it's a concrete or brick wall. Or maybe another barge or boat. Let's deal with the fixed wall first, since that is easier.

The fixed wall normally requires two items: a big tire and a bollard (or something to tie to). Place the tire between the bow and the wall to protect the barge's paint. If there is a stiff wind, the friction of the bow against the wall may not be enough to keep the bow from sliding sideways along it. Should that happen, secure a line from the forward barge bollard to any strong fixed object on or near the wall to hold the bow in place while you turn. The maneuver may require two tires and two lines. Hold the bow in place with one set while you re-secure the second set to another point on the boat with a better angle.

Let's focus on this maneuver for a moment. The closer you are able to secure the line to the center of the barge's bow, the better the angle for turning through most of the turn. Therefore, many barges have a flush mounted turning block, or pulley, on the rail between the forward bollards and the bow. The turning block allows the point of pull to be closer to the bow. To use it, secure the line to one of the bow bollards, then run it forward to the turning block before sending it shoreward.

Try to use the wind to help complete the turn. Depending on its direction, the wind can assist in several ways: to help bring the stern around, to move away from the bank after the turn, or even to blow the bow down in the direction of the turn.

It is absolutely critical to anticipate the entire turning maneuver before initiating. Visualize all the effects at each stage. Based on those effects, choose your tactics.

A few practices against a soft bank, or against a wall with appropriate protection and lines to hold you in case of heavy wind will give you the feel for this maneuver.

Turning against another barge or boat is much the same, except one is bound to be a little nervous pushing one's bow against another barge. Don't worry about being nervous, because you should be. After all, you don't want to scratch his hull, even though it is black (if he is a big commercial barge). Turning against a barge has the advantage of having bollards you can secure to if necessary. Make sure your crew has several tires available to cushion both the point of contact and the anticipated points of contact as your bow turns against his hull.

Now, as far as turning against a smaller boat is concerned, exercise great care. Consider your skill, any emergency, and the size of the boat compared to yours. The crackling of bursting fiberglass from that sharp little water ski boat somewhere under your bow can give nightmares.

Once again, how much hull is out of the water and exposed to the wind and how much hull is under the water giving greater stability will significantly affect a barge's turning ability. Let's leave the techniques used to stop and turn for a moment and examine more closely two physical aids used to assist a turn: ballast and bowthrusters.

Boiled to the essence, a choice frequently needs to be made between ballast and bowthrusters to provide control. We will take a brief look at both in the paragraphs below.

Assistance device: **Ballast**

Proper ballast has numerous advantages: directional stability, reduced susceptibility to cross wind, plus warmth in winter and reduced heat in

summer. It also establishes a new waterline and increases the life of the
hull. If the barge you are considering already has proper ballast, wonderful. If not, consider adding ballast.

On a charter the only way to add ballast, frankly, is to have your family pack heavily--real heavily. But for the owner, adding ballast is a serious option.

Most ballast is concrete, especially in boats converted more than 20
years ago. It is poured into the bottom of the hull before the interior is
finished. Proper pouring technique is essential to prevent condensation
between the concrete and the hull. Otherwise, virtually untreatable rusting will occur (see Chapter 10, *How to Buy the Right Barge*).

A second option to increase ballast is the use of fixed but movable
ballast, like large chunks of iron or steel or concrete.

A third option involves tankage. Adding water or fuel tankage will
immerse the hull more deeply in the water.

In sum, there are various options to add ballast to a barge. They may
be used singly or in combination, enabling you to achieve the advantages
of a properly ballasted boat. You may wish to investigate using a
bowthruster to give additional control in maneuvering, especially if you
are shy on ballast.

Assistance device: bowthruster

There is a saying among some professional barge skippers that a
bowthruster serves as a crutch for a lame skipper. On lightly ballasted
barges, however, a bowthruster can be very helpful. A bowthruster, by
moving the bow of the barge to one side or the other, gives the same
sideways control to the bow that rudder and torque give to the stern.
With a bowthruster, for example, a barge can turn on her own axis in
mid-canal without having to be so concerned about torque and momentum. Plus, a bowthruster helps bring the bow into the wind to complete a
U-turn, thus avoiding the bow-into-the-bank routine described above.

As a rule of thumb, for a lightly ballasted barge, consider a bowthruster. If well ballasted, disregard. In fact, a well ballasted boat would
have less room for a bowthruster. If the ballast is poured concrete, the
installation may have to circumvent the ballast.

Bowthrusters are controlled by a small swizzle stick in the pilothouse.
They are simple to operate. Push to port and the bow moves to port.

Push to starboard and the bow moves to starboard.   The simple part stops there.

Bowthrusters come in two types and many different sizes. If a barge is advertised as having a bowthruster, that should be the start of questions rather than an answer. Many bowthrusters, for instance, are woefully undersized. It can be like buying a Mack truck. Sure, it has an engine, but having a Volkswagen motor in a big semi won't do much good. The same is true for the size and power of bowthrusters.

Bowthrusters come in two versions: cylinders and propellers. Cylinders are for relatively small boats and propellers are for big barges. Unfortunately, there is a rather large gap in the middle which, of course, is where most cruising barges fall.

Cylinder type bowthrusters are actually large tubes that are installed athwartships in or under the bow of the barge below the waterline. A propeller, driven by an electric motor or by hydraulic pressure, is inserted in the middle of the tube. Operate the propeller screw one direction and the water pushes out the starboard side of the tube, moving the bow to port. Reverse the screw and the bow moves in the opposite direction. In practice, this type is most effective when the barge is either going very slow or stopped.   How effective depends on the power of the bowthruster. It also helps keep the bow straight when traveling in reverse.

The second type of bowthruster, the external propeller, functions much like the aft main propeller. It is smaller than the aft propeller, can be turned directionally, and can often be hydraulically withdrawn into the barge hull, much like an airplane's landing gear. Some large commercial barges have separate engines located forward that power the bowthruster screws. Others are hydraulically driven. Electric bowthrusters squeal like a captured pig when used.

How large a bowthruster is adequate? That depends upon a number of factors: weight of the barge, amount of ballast, area of exposed hull, and how strong a wind you want to be able to turn into. Either ask a knowledgeable boat surveyor or, if the barge under consideration already has a bowthruster installed, test it by U-turns in varying wind strengths, and note its effect when employed at different boat speeds. If you are considering having a bowthruster installed on your barge, make sure that you need one and that you precisely define what you want it to do. Then rely on the advice of the best two experts you can find, preferably experienced bargers and not salesmen.

Despite their significant cost and their limitations, bowthrusters can be a valuable assist in the right circumstances. They tend to be overrated, however, just as proper ballasting is underrated. Both will help with maneuvering, especially when the barge has little way (boat speed) and that is when you need help the most. Yet the most help will come from your own practiced knowledge of the principles we have discussed. You are on your way!

Chapter 4

MOORING

Mooring is simply tying off the vessel. Normal choices for mooring in Europe include walls, marinas, docks, banks, and anchoring. Before we address how to accomplish each type of mooring, it is important to focus on one basic element.

That basic element is this--a barge constantly moves unless securely tied down. I don't know what it is about barges, but they act like a nervous bull in a china closet. They are always on the move. Back and forth, in and out, to and fro. Granted, barges look like sleepers, but these looks are deceiving. There seems to be a lot of pent up energy in them, somewhat like an overgrown teenager who cannot sit still for a moment.

The barge may fool you at first. Tie her off and all looks well. But then she starts her quiet, nearly imperceptible rhythm: easy now, back and forth, back and forth, each back and each forth with a little more enthusiasm until a poorly secured tie becomes no tie at all.

When mooring a barge, treat her like a bull and tie down all four. Use at least four lines, and have them tight. The tighter the better. Use two bowlines and two stern lines. Lead two lines forward and two aft.

Two of the lines should pretty much hold the barge where you want her. These, a bowline and a stern line, preferably leading away from the barge (the bowline leading slightly forward, the sternline slightly aft) should be the first secured to the shore.

The remaining two lines are used as "springs". These are the ones that tie down the bull and keep him from charging back and forth-- prevent him from "springing" forward or "springing" aft. The springs should be longer than the bow and stern lines and normally should be led from the ends of the barge toward the middle, where they are secured to something on shore. These two lines function as shock absorbers. They must be tight enough to hold the bull down.

stern line   spring lines   bow line

You will find that mooring lines stretch, especially the springs. Periodic tensioning is often necessary to keep her under good control. Of course, the tighter the lines at the outset, the less tensioning later. For now, let's turn our attention to securing the boat end of the mooring line.

For those who are used to cranking in on sailboat winches--forget it. No such thing on barges. Bollards don't turn. You have to be clever instead. There are some parallels, however. As on winches, take at least three wraps around the bollard for adequate line/bollard friction before securing. Make wraps clockwise.

At the end of the third wrap, lead the line over one ear of the bollard, then bring it back and tie it off on the other ear, using a simple half hitch; the line should head up toward you from the half hitch.

half hitch

An alternative to the half hitch is an intentional overwrap. After the three wraps, make a loop and twist it so that the line rides over itself as it lays above the ears on the boat bollard. The greater the pull on the mooring line, the tighter the loop holds itself. In our experience, however, the half hitch is easier to tie, more reliable, and easier to untie after tension.

Normally on a barge, two bollards are located side by side. This allows several options. As discussed under locks, you can place the loop end around one boat bollard, lead the line around the lock bollard and then secure the line using the second boat bollard. Or, if you are mooring and the loop end is on the shore, you can use the first bollard as a partial friction brake before taking the three wraps on the second bollard. This often enables you to hold the tension better after giving a firm tug on the line as you prepare to take your wraps.

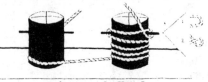

using two bollards

After mooring, check the lines to assure they will not chafe. If they rub on a portion of the barge or on a jutting portion of the dock or wall, they may easily chafe through during the night. Protect them with a cloth or plastic bag wrapped at the chafe point.

Next morning, check the lines for tautness. They may well have loosened as the lines stretch and may need another tug to take up the tension.

Watch the barge as you take up tension. If the lines are somewhat loose, the barge will be moving somewhat to and fro, surging and receding. Take up line tension when the boat movement is at maximum in your favor. Going with the flow sure beats trying to wrestle tons of steel.

There are two exceptions to the rule of mooring lines being tight. The first is in tidal areas where the water level may rise or fall. Too much tension on the mooring lines will cause the barge to either hang up or become slightly submerged.

Mooring in rivers with a fairly strong current is the second exception. First, the river, responding to rain and snow melt, may change its level. Second, the current exerts constant pressure on the barge, canceling the to and fro surging. In these cases a comfortable slack is appropriate.

Before we leave the subject of spring lines, I should describe another phenomenon of barging that demands that spring lines be extended as long as possible. We discovered it the hard way, after having stopped along a broad canal in eastern Friesland (northwest province of the Netherlands) to visit relatives. The boys secured the four mooring lines into the dirt bank, setting two with land anchors and two with pins. We hopped on our folding bikes and headed off through the fertile fields to surprise our distant relation.

We were the ones surprised, however, as on our return late that evening we found a pin and an anchor torn out of the ground, lying there lazy-like, as if someone had pulled them out for the fun of it. Indeed, that is what we suspected. How else could these securely buried hunks of steel end up lying on the grassy bank? Chagrined, we reburied them and, content our barge was well secured, went to bed.

I was awakened the next morning by a strange sensation that all was not well. As I clambered from bed, 14-year-old Justin yelled, *"Dad, we're loose! We're floating down the canal!!"*

Rushing to the window, I saw water where the bank had been. Yes, we were totally adrift in the canal, dangerously angled to block any passing multi-thousand ton barge that might happen by!

Your thought is the same as mine. Heedless of the proprieties of suitable attire, I scampered to the pilothouse to look for the looming hulks of any of those canal giants. I saw one, but he was receding into the distance. Instantly, I directed my now awake crew into action. They retrieved the dragging mooring lines, still attached to the now wet steel pins and anchors, as I retrieved my trousers. I started the engine and we got off to one of our quicker starts of the cruise.

Careful analysis and subsequent experience leads to the following 20-20 hindsight of what happened, both the previous evening and on our morning adrift. What had pulled out our secured land anchors and pins was not a passing prankster, but instead, passing barges. As we will see in Chapter 6 *Meeting and Overtaking*, passing barges cause a pushing bow wave followed by a pulling suction as their prop draws water. This is followed by a push again as the propeller spews water out the stern. This push-pull-push sequence has a significant effect on your barge as it meets another on the canal. It has even more significance if you are moored at the side of the canal. The push of the passing barge wants to rip the lines out of the bank. The suction caused by the prop is even more pronounced. Its pull is not only opposite the preceding push, it also tries to pull the barge away from the bank and into itself. It is perfectly natural--a hungry propeller demands to be fed and pulls water from wherever it can get it--from the front and from the sides. At the sides it will draw the water in at an angle from the banks. If your barge is at the bank, it gets pulled as well.

There is another action that occurs at this moment which adds a twist to the passing barge's effort to tear your vessel from her moorings. The big barge, sucking water to feed her prop, actually draws down the water level, lowering your barge even as she pulls it. All told, you get a bow wave push, followed by a pulling in and down, followed by a raising water level push. No wonder our pins and anchors wrenched free.

The power of the wrenching effect is directly related to barge speed and underwater volume. No--more than directly related, its effect is exponential. If a barge backs off on the RPM as she approaches, even though going quite fast, it is much easier on your moored barge. The same is true if the barge goes by slowly but under power. The worst case by far is a fully loaded barge continuing, in gear, full power, right on by you. Look out!

The effects of this are far reaching and often surprising. We had moored for several months during the winter on a little tributary of Germany's Neckar River called the Elsenz, in the quaint village of Neckargemund. Tucked up in this modest stream, we considered ourselves immune to river barges. Not so. Though we were moored several hundred yards (OK, *meters*; it's Europe) from the river, and though the Neckar is very broad and deep in this section, when a barge ran the river, we dropped at least a foot! The huge propellers on those massive barges sucked so much water that the little stream nearly drained. Ducks and swans would suddenly swoosh downstream toward the river. They were accustomed to it though, as they waited patiently for the propeller push of the stern wave to shove them back upstream. Meanwhile, our barge would bottom out on the stream bank and list a bit until the stern wave brought us level again. That's the power of the big barges.

There was a speed limit on that specific section of the Neckar for precisely that reason. If the barges slowed, even somewhat, we would only drop a few inches. But when a big one came barreling through at top speed, over we would go.

Because we were moored there so long, we got to be quite expert at this exercise. Before a barge even came into view, we could tell whether or not this was a loaded speeder. All would be calm and then suddenly, swish! It was less like someone pulling the plug in a bathtub and more like putting a giant wet-vac hose into a bucket. We discovered that the human nature of barge drivers is much like car drivers: they observe the speed limit if they think they might get caught. The barge drivers knew that the German water police didn't patrol heavily until after six or seven. Morning after morning, about five o'clock, I would awake with the premonition of "*Here it comes again!*". Sure enough, some barge would be blasting through while the *Polizei* slept, and our barge leaned down the suddenly waterless bank, rolling me onto my wife and sometimes tipping over a flower vase.

Of course, the drop in the water level was accompanied by a massive current outflow which tugged mightily at our mooring lines, stretching them regularly. Just as regularly, we took up the slack every few days.

Fine, you say, *I understand the problem and its cause, how can I prevent it? Is it possible to keep the pins and land anchors in the bank in the face of a barge gone ballistic?* Maybe. It depends on the weight of the barge, the speed, and the depth and breadth of the waterway. But yes, there are keys to keeping yourself tied to the bank.

The keys are three words: *long, close,* and *tight.* Focus primarily on the spring lines here, because these are the two that act as the fore and aft shock absorbers. The bow and stern lines must be tight also, to keep the barge against the bank, and set at a slight angle to counteract the away-from-the-bank pull of the prop's sucking action. But the main thing is the springs. Whenever you anticipate a potential wrestling match with passing barges, such as mooring along an open stretch of commercial canal, make the spring lines long, at least 3/4 of your vessel's length, longer if possible. The longer the line, the more stretch, or, put another way, the greater the shock absorber effect. Too short and the jolt from the passing barge will yank your mooring device right out of the bank.

Secondly, run the spring lines as near and as parallel to the boat as you can. Set the land anchor or pin as close to the boat as possible, consistent with setting in solid holding ground. That way, when your barge surges fore and aft, the tug on the mooring device will be as straight as possible. The greater the angle of pull away from the barge, the sooner it will pull out, especially with land anchors, which we will discuss in more detail in a moment.

Thirdly, and probably most importantly, make the line tight; super snug. Often, you can use the motor to get good tension on the springs. First put the transmission in forward and stretch the first spring forward while the crew ties off the other spring. Then place her in reverse to set the opposite spring.

When shallow water or rocks near the bank endanger the prop, crew muscle must substitute for engine power. Have the crew put a real "*heave ho*" as they bring that spring tight.

The most effective "*heave ho*" is ninety degree mechanical advantage. First, pull the line as tight as possible, bend it halfway around one boat bollard and temporarily secure it with a wrap around an ear of the second boat bollard. Then put physics to work. Have a crew member ashore grab the mooring line in its middle and pull perpendicularly. This will both tighten the line as well as draw the barge close to shore, both desirable. On cue, the crew releases the line as you quickly--very quickly-- take up the slack. Do this two or three times and you can play a violin concerto on the mooring line.

The reason for strong tension is probably obvious to you: It keeps the barge tied down and prevents the buildup of momentum that, if allowed, triples and quadruples the power of the pull on the lines.

In sum, the three keys for setting spring lines in a vulnerable situation are long, close, and tight.

MOORING EQUIPMENT

Bollards and rings are preferred; when they are not available, use the pins and land anchors that you carry with you.

Bollards are commonly found on the top of lock walls (though you will seldom if ever tie off for the night here) and on top of city walls. They are shaped like a fine lady's figure, and you lay the line or loop around the waist. **Rings** are frequently set into the side of a wall, secured by a pin, though sometimes they lie on top of a city wall as well. Both devices are excellent to tie to.

Avoid ring chafe if at all possible. A ring, because of its sharp contour, will wear more rapidly through a mooring line than a bollard. A quiet moorage is one thing, but with passing traffic or wakes, the surge on the lines can eat right through an improperly tied line.

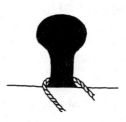

bollard

A line from the barge bollard to the shore and then back again can chafe against the ring in a surge. Instead, use the loop end of the line to tie off on shore. Tie off on the ring using one of two methods: a "cowboy lasso" or a steel bar. To tie onto a ring with a "cowboy lasso", bring the loop end of the mooring line through the ring. Then pass the rest of the line through the loop. Draw it up tight like a cowboy lasso so this knot of sorts is up against the ring with no possibility of line movement against the steel.

It is quicker and easier to use a steel bar. Again, bring the loop end of the mooring line up through the ring. Insert the bar through the loop and tension the line. The line now pulls against the bar and the ring. Because it is so easily loosened, I don't advise this for long periods or insecure areas.

When there is no bollard or ring, look around for something else solid, but please heed this caution. There are several mooring no-no's. Do not tie to trees, fence posts, or kilometer stones. Trees are generally illegal to tie to throughout Europe, understandably so. The chafe can cut through the bark and injure the tree. Germans are so serious about this (Germans love trees more than any people I know) that a Heidelberg professor we met who lives along the Neckar River was given a hefty fine for tying his own boat to his own tree in his own back yard! Fence posts belong to the farmer adjacent to the canal and are not strong enough to hold a barge; especially in Holland where a light force can pull the fence post out of the soft, rich soil. Kilometer markers--huge white stones about two foot cubed--line many of Europe's canals but are set shallowly and are not intended for mooring.

How do you moor when no bollard, rings, or other suitable substitutes are available? Carry your own mooring devices. Pins and land anchors are the most common. Use pins to secure bow and stern lines, and land anchors for springs.

Pins normally are solid steel cylinders two to three feet long, with a looped handle on top to push the pin into the ground and extract it again. Angle the bottom tip a little toward the boat as you push it in to provide a firmer hold. A small sledge helps for tough ground but avoid heavy blows which will

mooring pin

gradually flatten the looped handle. The screw pin presents a suitable alternative though I have not seen one with thick enough steel to handle the surging thrusts imposed by a passing barge.

A land anchor looks like a thin, underweight sea anchor, or an over-weight giant fish hook. Set these first. Attach the mooring line to the ring at the end of the anchor stock. Again, use the cowboy lasso knot to avoid chafe. Here is a short cut for your lasso knot--instead of putting the rest of the mooring line through the loop end, simply guide the loop end through the ring, and then keep the loop going until it is over the entire land anchor. Pass the land anchor through the loop and draw the loop back to the ring. Voila!--a nifty lasso knot!

Land anchor

Now that the line is properly attached to the ring of the land anchor, the crew should lead the anchor to where you want it buried (nearly parallel and long), plus another two or three feet. They need the extra distance to set the anchor. Secure the other end of the line around the boat bollard. The crew member should face you while he or she pushes down on the anchor as you engage the transmission and power forward or back, depending on which spring you are setting. The barge will pull the hook part of the anchor--called a fluke--down into the soil, leaving only the stock and ring exposed, which will lie flat along the top of the ground. It is really a slick little maneuver and works well. Be sure, however, that your crew "aims" the stock of the anchor toward the boat bollard to which the other end of the spring line is secured so that the direction of pull on the land anchor is straight. If it is not, the land anchor will slip sideways and quite easily pull out of the soil. After setting the first land anchor, set the second.

There are two ways to pull out a land anchor upon departure. If the bank is nicely maintained, perhaps with mown grass, as many of them are, release the line from the barge bollard and grab the handle at the working end of the stock.   Pull it up and away from the boat, as if you were extracting a hook from the mouth of a fish. This technique leaves the earth relatively undisturbed. Should the ground be too tough for this to work, simply lift up on the ring. This leverage will bring up the fluke quickly. Tamp the disturbed soil to resemble its original appearance.

It is also possible to use lengths of 5cm x 5cm angle iron sawed to a point at one end. They should be hammered into the ground at an angle, away from the direction of pull. This requires a big hammer, of course.

The combination of pins for the bow and stern lines, and land anchors for the springs, will hold well in most situations. They provide a wonderful versatility, allowing one to moor virtually whenever the spirit so moves (or stops)--an essential part of the cruising lifestyle. Besides, it also means free moorage.

MOORING PLACES

Canal Banks

This is by far the most common means of mooring in most smaller canals. Larger canals often run commercial traffic 24 hours a day, which can make mooring a little hazardous, given the push-pull-tug described earlier. With firm soil on the bank, however, you can try mooring on the larger canals; just keep a close eye on the lines as the first few big barges test your mooring ability.

On many smaller canals in Holland, the Dutch have installed little wooden docks in the countryside, complete with little wood pilings for the bank and a plank on top. Small bollards and rings are often on or near the plank. Primarily intended for smaller craft, barge skippers need to tie gently to avoid damage. These areas are denoted by a small red bollard mark on the excellent Dutch canal charts.

Most often, however, you will just pick a nice spot to pull to the side and stop for the night. Avoid parking on curves where your presence may come as a surprise to other traffic.

Now comes the fun part: the mooring maneuver. Read this slowly as you envision each step in this process. After you pick the spot, slow down, and assure that the crew has ground tackle ready for use--lines coiled and ready to run free (but make sure the crew never steps in the coil or allows the line near the steering mechanism), pins and land anchors at the ready. An approach to port works best with a right hand turning prop, as you know from chapter 2 on *Torque*. Designate a crew member to jump ashore. (I hesitate to advise someone to jump to a mooring, since normally jumping needs to be avoided. It is dangerous in all but a very, very few instances, soft canal banks being one of them.) Gradually angle at slow speed into the bank so that the port bow shoulder, the shallowest part of the craft, eases into the bank. From there the crew jumps ashore, either with line and land anchor in hand or having thrown the line with land anchor already attached, to the bank before they jump.

Now you are stopped, or nearly so. Secure the bow line to the shore, leading it from the bow to as far aft on the shore as is practical, so it can act as a spring line. Set the land anchor. Once the bow is secured, bring the stern in by slipping the transmission in forward, ever so gently, out of respect for the shallow waters--and possible rocks--near the bank. Good! Patiently now, watch your work of art as the barge gently sidles up to the bank. Of course, your hand is always on the transmission during this phase, ready to instantly bring it to neutral in case the propeller hits a rock, a hunk of buried wood, or the canal bottom. The rest is simple. Set the other spring line.

If you have extra crew, have them hold bow and stern lines ashore while the springs are being set. Be extra careful using reverse gear to set the land anchor forward because reverse torque will press the stern more firmly into the bank, with greater risk of propeller damage. With the springs set tightly, push the pins into the bank, at a slight angle away from the barge, with the lines led at about a 45 degree angle forward from the bow and aft from the stern bollards.

As skipper, double check the security of the pins and land anchors ashore, and the way the mooring lines are tied to the boat bollards. Yes, I have had experienced crew tie off on a bollard and then have it work loose. If the barge comes loose, it is the skipper's responsibility, not the crew's. With lines secure, the barge is set for the night. Depending on the distance to the bank, you may wish to run the barge's wooden walking plank to the land. Place a cloth where it rests on the barge's painted surface.

In France, land of many locks, the location of your evening mooring may be determined for you when the lockkeeper goes home, which may vary by the time of year. At least you know there will be no disturbance from passing barges during the night.

Walls

Cities usually line the rivers and canals that pass through them with walls quite a bit higher than the normal water level as a precaution against flooding. This is especially true in the mountainous areas of Germany and France. Sometimes one can tie to bollards at the top of the wall. Otherwise look for bollards set into the wall or rings secured to the wall.

Where there are tall walls, there are also, frequently, ladders. Look for one and with luck you may be able to position the barge for both a good mooring as well as ladder access.

Mooring along walls requires innovation to run spring lines properly. Instead of the spring lines crossing neatly within your boat length, for example, they may run forward of the bow and aft of the stern, considerably extending your mooring area. The effect, however, is largely the same.

Another trick that helps keep the bow and stern neatly tucked tightly against the wall is to run the bow and stern lines from the boat's outboard bollards instead of those nearest the wall. For example, if moored to port, run the bow and stern lines from the starboard bollards. It makes the angle of pull more wall-ward, and less fore and aft, that function being performed by the springs.

Your approach to the wall will be more parallel than the canal bank approach. Here, the goal is to come to a stop just as the barge is directly alongside the wall. Designate a crew with a mobile fender (tire) just in case the approach is a bit less than perfect.

Once you are quite experienced at barge handling, you may wish to try the mid-ship bollard technique, especially if you are short on crew. It is very convenient but requires finesse on the controls. Your barge needs to be nearly parallel the wall and stopped. As you stand next to the midship bollards, place the loop end of the mooring line around the wall's bollard or through the ring. (Use the boat hook if you are a few feet away). Engage the transmission in idle forward. After the barge has moved forward about one quarter of its length, gradually tension the line around the midship bollards. Once secured and taut, the engine will keep the barge snugly against the wall while you and your crew secure the bow and stern lines. This technique is particularly convenient if your pilothouse is amidships.

Finally, you may encounter situations that require "advanced parallel parking techniques". (Try this only after significant experience handling your barge.) Imagine, for example, that rows of barges have rafted together—four or five deep—along a wall. Then, a distance just over your barge length back, another group of barges has rafted, leaving you a deeply inset parking spot, if you can get your barge into that parallel parking situation. How to do it?

Don't back in as you would a car. On the contrary, your turning mechanism, unlike the car's, is at the back of the barge (the rudder). So go in bow first. Approach **very** slowly. Remember the momentum factor discussed in Chapter 3, *Stopping and Turning*. Point the bow about one meter aft of its final moored location. When the bow is a meter or two from the wall, swing the rudder over hard to begin bringing your stern in. You don't need to get it in all the way, but as much as you can given the tightness of the parallel park. Put crew ashore as the bow gently nudges the wall, with line in hand. The other end of the line should be attached to the bow bollard.

You are now stopped and the crew should secure the other end of the line to shore anywhere aft of the bow, the further aft the better. By the time the line is secured, your barge may have drifted away from the wall. No problem. Gradually take up the slack on the line as you engage forward. Once taut, your barge will move sideways, ever so gently, until you are snugged against the wall. By the way, this technique works just as well if you are rafting against another barge deeply inset, instead of the wall.

Incidentally, one of the delights of cruising European waterways is that, given their history, cities sprang up along the routes of commerce—the waterways. So nearly all cities and towns that amount to anything, especially the old historic ones, lie along some canal or river. This is particularly true in lowland countries where canal building was less arduous and often performed the dual function of land drainage as well as transportation. So walls abound.

So do "parking attendants", in some cities, who come to collect over-night moorage fees, even though they offer no facilities and the watercraft are moored in public waterways. The Dutch are the most enthusiastic collectors for their city coffers, and generally charge around a Guilder (more or less 65 cents) per meter of length per night. Of course, for those on the frugal side, nothing prevents mooring in the city during the day to explore it, then heading just outside the city to run lines ashore into the bank at no charge.

Two words of caution regarding mooring on walls: *safety* and *changing water levels*. Steel, concrete, or masonry walls are very unforgiving of human limbs placed between them and several tons of steel barge. Caution the crew to keep hands and feet inboard and to never lean out or jump. Much better to make another approach or sand and paint over a scrape on the hull.

The second caution relates to mooring along river walls where sea tides, or wind in the lowlands, or rain and snow melt can affect the level of the river. Refer to the section on mooring in rivers and tidal areas later in this chapter.

Docks

Docks are as scarce as they are ideal. They are easy to tie to but diffi-cult to find except in marinas.

Marinas

Barges are usually too big to fit in most marinas, which are designed for sport boats. In reality, that is an advantage, since people realize your size prevents you from going in the marinas and they don't expect you to be there. If, however, you very much want to be in a marina and pay the extra charges for doing so you usually can maneuver yourself in, with dexterity. Be extremely cognizant of speed. Most marina floats in Europe are constructed of aluminum. It feels like tying to a tin can.

Marinas offer showers, 220 volt shorepower, and sometimes other amenities. Prices range from the equivalent of $1/meter length in some areas of Holland to upwards of $4/meter at the "Arsenal" in Paris. Be-cause of the danger of flooding on the rivers and freezing on the canals, many marina docks are moved onto land in late fall, not to return until spring.

Tying off in the marina will depend on the situation. Just remember the principles of holding the bow and stern in place and using spring lines to prevent fore and aft movement.

AT NIGHT, SET A LIGHT

Whenever moored for the night where there may be nocturnal traffic on the water, set a light. The proper place is outboard of the pilothouse. Use an electric light or a lantern. We used my son's little red kerosene lantern, which worked just fine except in high winds. Of course, when the locks and bridges are closed and no one can transit at night (as in most French canals), there is no need to post the night light. Always set the light on rivers and large canals, unless in a marina.

Incidentally, don't even *think* of cruising at night. To do so requires radar, years of experience, exceptional knowledge of the local waterways, and a prayer. Your barge should be equipped with night navigation lights for use in emergencies--know where they are and test them-- but leave them strictly for emergencies.

If you doubt my caution, stand on the deck some dark night on a city waterway. Watch the lights on shore--or are they reflecting off the water?--and imagine trying to pick out a slow moving red or green light moving toward you. Now try to make out the bank....

MOORING IN RIVERS AND TIDAL AREAS

Fortunately, tidal canals are usually oxymoronic--virtually a contradiction of terms. There may be one somewhere but I don't know of it. Obviously, the tidal swells would suck it to the sea on a low tide and push it landward on the flood. Locks control that sort of thing.

Of course, wherever there is water, there are intriguing phenomena. Take western Overijssel for instance, a Dutch province northeast of the Ijsselmeer where the canals spread in a neat network. Strong southwesters blow from the English channel, roll over the lowland tulip fields north of Amsterdam and onto the shallow Ijsselmeer, the largest inland body of water in the Netherlands. This was the Zuider Zee before it became a fresh water lake by construction of the great *Aufsluitdyk*. The

Ijsselmeer averages about ten feet of depth. As experienced boaters know, strong wind stacks such shallow water into a steep chop. The three to five foot choppy waves form resistance to the southwest wind, which actually shoves the water--tons of it--out of the Ijsselmeer and up the feeding rivers and canals to the northeast. The Ijssel River and the large Zwartewater Canal will rise, sometimes by as much as six feet in a big blow! The Dutch have constructed storm gates on the smaller canals off the Zwartewater to prevent inundation of most of the rich farmland. If protected by a storm gate in such conditions, the barge may only experience a one or two foot rise. But if tied to the Kampen wall along the river Ijssel, or along the Zwartewater Canal in Hasselt, one will need to take precautions.

The other caution occurs in rivers which are subject to flooding, or, in areas close to the sea, to tidal effect. We rode the ebb tide as Belgium's River Schelde emptied into the sea, seemingly careening down the river-bed at almost twice our normal speed over ground. It was a great ride until the tide turned and we had to climb against the surging flood. At full power we inched ahead, uncertain at one point if we would make it or if we would have to await the turning of the tide once again. The water level change on that river can exceed ten feet. Obviously one does not moor along it unless on a floating dock or in a nice flat tributary that dries at high tide.

Tides, except when affected by wind, are predictable, both in level and in time. Tide tables or local authorities can predict the changes throughout the night. You can calculate the rise or fall from the state of the tide at the moment.

European rivers are subject to flooding. Given all the dams and locks on the rivers, I found the flooding surprising. Our first real exposure to that occurred on Germany's Neckar River which passes through such cities as Stuttgart and Heidelberg before joining the Rhine at Mannheim.

We tied to a seemingly perfectly placed masonry wall in the charming little city of Eberbach, which sits like a sparkling jewel against the steep-sided river gorge. The top of the river wall was just below the level of the barge's coachroof, giving us lots of light below and almost a view of the city from the cabin. The locals spoke of "*Hochwasser*" and, near December, "*Adventhochwasser*"--Christmas high water, or flooding. With snow on the hillsides, they said, a heavy warm rain could send the river over the dams in a matter of hours. It sobered our thoughts. We continued up the river to the KWO nuclear power plant, dining with its president and wife, the Danglemaiers, in a restaurant ("*Gasthaus*") quite far up from the river. They related how the dining room in which we ate had been immersed in an "*Adventhochwasser*". It drove the point home. A few weeks later we made our way back down river. We stopped once again at picturesque Eberbach and tied up to the convenient masonry wall. Casually, a local acquaintance remarked that it was a good thing we were not moored there a few days before. "*Why?*", we asked. Because flooding had completely covered the entire wall, even covering the adjacent parking lot!

How could that be?, we wondered. We had been on that same Neckar River during that period and hadn't noticed a thing. The reason? We had been moored at the time of the flooding at Besigheim, another of our favorite Neckar towns, but the reason we did not notice the flooding was that we were moored just *above* the lock. The change in the water level during floods, we learned, is far greater below a dam than above it. The lesson: whenever "*Hochwasser*" hits, or might hit, tie to the dock approaches of the lock—on the **upstream** side of the lock.

Well, you ask, *if we know the water level may change during the night, what do we do about it?*

First, when mooring on a river, always moor with the bow pointed upstream. Even if the river current is very slow, do not tie with the stern into the current.

Second, lengthen mooring lines to their absolute maximum. String them out as far as possible so they can absorb a change in water level without binding the boat.

Third, determine if the level will likely rise or fall. With predictable tides that is easy. Before or after a big rainstorm on a river, it will be more difficult. Then try to tie onto points ashore that will be close to but definitely above the anticipated new water level.

In some cases, one must move. If we were tied to the Eberbach wall when the flood hit, for example, the danger would have been mooring in the parking lot. We either would have had to move up or down stream to the nearest high side approach to a lock, or we would have had to place tall uprights along the wall so we would not float into the parking lot.

The best technique for flooding I saved until last: tie to a commercial barge, after getting permission from the skipper. He is more experienced, knows what he is doing, and best of all, he becomes a floating dock.

ANCHORING

One may anchor in a large bay-type harbor like Enkhuizen's north harbor on the Ijsselmeer, or in a lake like the *Beulaker Wijde* in Netherland's Overijssel Province.

Or, be adventuresome and leave the well-marked deeper channels of the saltwater Wadden Zee at high tide, anchor and wait for the tide to change. Ringing the curving northwest coastline of Friesland, this five to seven mile wide belt of water is in turn ringed by the long, stretched out string of Friesian Islands that acts as a giant provincial breakwater protecting the mainland from the fierce waters of the North Sea. Do not be misled, however, during high winds the shallow waters of the Wadden Zee pile up in steep rows of waves just like the Ijsselmeer--not conditions for barges.

The Wadden Zee, except for the dredged channels cut through the sandy bottom, dries at low tide. Want to inspect your bottom or do some hull painting? The flat bottomed barge will rest conveniently on the drying sand, to be lifted again in a few hours when the twice daily flood fills in. It is a fun and novel experience; but make a careful weather check before venturing from Harlingen or the lock at the north end of the Aufsluitdyk.

You will be tempted to anchor in one of Holland's gravel or peat lakes. Many of the lakes in the north are turf lakes, named for the deep layers of peat extracted as a home heat source for centuries before the discovery of petroleum and natural gas. Because Holland lacks the forests of France or Germany, wood was a scarce commodity for either building or burning, and the Dutch kept warm in winter by literally burning the earth under them, at least the peat earth. (No, that's not why they are now below sea level!) The hardy Dutch pulled the soggy peat into little barges, then drained, dried, and shipped it to homes where it was burned in "Dutch ovens" for cooking and heating. The legacy of peat mining is found in the wine-colored waters of the lakes and small canals of these peat regions.

In more modern times, the development of cement brought demand for gravel. In response, Holland has created gravel lakes as a by-product of gravel extraction. The process continues, especially in the south along the Maas River where the tiny stones from the French and Belgian Ardennes have been washed by the waters of time into lowland deposits, now being mined and converted into recreational lakes.

The gravel lakes have steeper banks than the turf lakes, which prompts a slightly different form of berthing than we Americans are accustomed to. Boats and barges line the shore, bows pushed into the beach and sterns pointed into the lake. Of course, one can anchor in such lakes, but putting bows on the shore accommodates many more boats and leaves the center of the lake for fishing, sailing, and water skiing. Neat idea.

This mooring technique is quite simple.

First, check the wind direction before choosing a beach. Top choice is a windward shore; second is a leeward shore. Problems can occur with a heavy side wind.

Second, choose a suitable spot, probably between some beached boats.

Third, pretend you are an LST making a landing at Normandy--head straight for the shore, but at a very slow speed.

Fourth, have a crew member with gloves stand in the stern ready to throw the emergency (stern) anchor overboard. The line must be properly coiled and ready to run free. Assure the crew member stands well outside of the coil. About 50-75 feet from the shore (depending on the length of the emergency anchor rode), as your barge glides toward shore, instruct the crew to toss the anchor (they should keep sufficient line tension to keep it free of the prop).

Now momentum gently nudges the barge onto the gravelly beach. Put the engine in forward gear at idle to keep the bow snugged into the shore. Crew should now disembark with a couple of pins and mooring lines spread in a "V" shape from the bow or mid ship bollards to the shore to keep the bow aground and to keep it from shifting sideways. Then kill the engine, tension the emergency anchor rode slightly, and you are set. Some folks mark the location of their stern anchor with a float and line attached before tossing it overboard.

Probably the greatest caution here is one I alluded to earlier: a strong side wind can stretch the rode and push the stern sideways. To a certain extent you can anticipate this by setting the anchor at an angle into the wind. If the situation worsens, move to a portion of the beach with a better wind angle.

To date we haven't used the ship's primary anchor when beaching, though some commercial barges do. It takes training, practice, and technique to let go the anchor at precisely the right moment of approach, let it pass under most of the barge while avoiding the danger of fouling the propeller, and secure the bow tightly at the proper angle to shore. It is a marvel to watch. But let's examine more conventional anchoring with the primary hook.

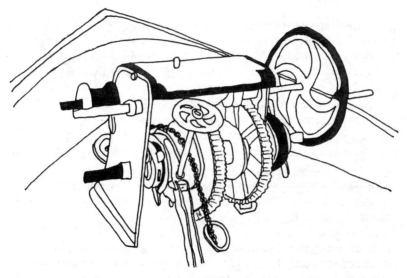

anchor windlass

On barges the primary rode is normally chain. It is heavy, lies on the bottom of the lake, and, by keeping the angle of tug on the anchor at lake bottom level, gives excellent holding power on short scope. Because of the tremendous weight of chain and anchor, mechanical advantage is a must for raising anchor. On barges, the old fashioned windlass is both stylish and practical.

Before you anchor in open water, check the wind direction, the weather forecast, and the chain (to assure it can run free).

Head into the wind and select the desired anchor spot. Check the water depth with a stick if there is no depth sounder because many of the lakes are very shallow. Make sure that a 360 degree rotation around the anchor caused by an overnight change in wind direction will cause neither you nor other boats harm. If other boats at anchor are using a single anchor, do likewise. If they have deployed the stern anchor to prevent swing, do the same. The goal is to avoid bumps in the night.

When over the desired anchor spot, stop the boat completely. Next, release the screw brake on the windlass. One of the two brakes on the windlass, the screw brake is a wheel with about four outward pointing spoke-like ears located right next to the "gypsy" or sprocket on which the chain lies as it passes through the windlass on its way from the anchor to its below-decks storage. This wheel type brake rides on a threaded axle. Turn it one direction and it threads away from the gypsy; rotate it the other direction and it sidles snug up against the gypsy. Get it snug enough and the friction keeps the gypsy from rotating. Tap the screw brake's ears so the brake rotates away from the gypsy, so the gypsy can run free. A few light taps usually break it free and then you can move it easily.

But the anchor still does not drop. That is because the steering wheel brake also must be loosened. I call it a steering wheel brake because it has what looks like a little steering wheel on a shaft. The shaft leads to a band that clasps the axle like a stretch-type wristwatch band. Turn the steering wheel to the right and it clasps the axle tightly. Turn it to the left and it releases its grip on the axle, allowing it to "free wheel" like a car that rolls down the hill with the clutch all the way to the floor.

So you turn the little steering wheel to the left and wait expectantly.... One of two events will now occur. Either the anchor will drop or it won't. If it doesn't, *carefully* give the shaft of the anchor an encouraging shove with the heel of your shoe. If that does not work, double check that both brakes are loose and then return to the anchor. Pretend you are in front of a Coke machine that won't give you a coke or return your money. Presto! The rapid rumble of chain lets you know the anchor is on its way to the bottom.

If the chain keeps running after the anchor is on the bottom, slowly tighten the steering wheel brake just until the chain stops. Return to the cabin and slip the transmission gently into reverse. The chain will play out as you slip slowly backward. When you have let out sufficient chain (scope), tighten both brakes and make sure the little finger stop on the bracket gear is in place. That prevents the windlass works from turning, which would of course allow the chain to continue to run. As the brakes tighten, the chain will slow as the reverse momentum of the barge sets the anchor. You can rest well.

How much chain should you let out? That depends on the depth of the water and the expected weather conditions. The greater the depth, the lighter the ballast, and the worse the wind, the greater the scope needed. On a typical mild summer night in the seemingly eternal shallow waters of Holland's lakes (seldom deeper than 6 to 10 feet) we would rest very easy with about a boat length of chain on the bottom.

How do you know how much chain is out? Some people tie a plastic bottle or a fender and line to the anchor to mark its location, thereby visually estimating the scope. Others will paint chain links white: one white link at one fathom (six feet), two white links at two fathoms, and so on.

To raise the anchor, make sure the little finger-like catch is on the gear (as it should have been after you set the anchor). That way the anchor will not fall back to the bottom if you stop to rest. Next, tap the screw brake loose again so the sprocket-like gypsy can turn in response to the big windlass wheel. Don't touch the little steering wheel. You want that to stay tight so the free wheeling is stopped and the big windlass wheel is "in gear" as you turn it and wind up the chain. This is good exercise, because you are literally pulling your barge through the water toward the anchor. You may wish to slowly idle in forward gear so the chain is slightly--but only slightly--slack. After all, you don't want to run over the chain and have it catch in the prop.

Once the anchor clears the water, stop for a moment to clean the anchor with brush and water bucket before hoisting it tightly into storage. When it is drawn up properly, all the way up and tight, rotate the screw brake snugly against the gypsy and give it a few authoritative taps with a bar as insurance. Then double check that the steering wheel brake is tight to the right and that the little anti-reverse finger is on the gear. The importance of these double checks becomes obvious if you envision the anchor suddenly releasing as you are mid-canal at full cruising speed.

I strongly recommend testing the anchor assembly before you get underway with your barge the very first time--and make sure all your crew is there watching. Should the engine fail, the anchor can become an important emergency device that needs to be released very quickly by any crew on deck.

It can happen. When we replaced the quaint and lovable but inadequate 1922 single cylinder Kromhout with a powerful DAF motor, we temporarily removed the day fuel tank in order to drop in the new engine. Of course, during the process the tank was bounced and shaken a bit. It had also been around for perhaps 70 years, not always full, and rust had formed along the interior walls. Lots of rust. But neither we nor the installing yard thought to check the interior of this well-maintained tank with its brightly painted exterior. After we installed the new engine, we re-installed the spiffy looking day tank and made an enjoyable short trek from Zwartsluis to Kampen--an uneventful one.

On the return trip the breeze piped up from the west over the Ijsselmeer, sending lacy-white pipecurls up the Ijssel River. We motored downstream, directly into the building breeze before cutting to the right behind a headland and into a willowstick-marked channel which guided us through the flooded flats on either side. The breeze now blew from our ten o'clock. The barge surged gently through the scudding chop.

Suddenly the engine coughed, sputtered, and starved out. Thinking I had inadvertently left the fuel valve closed, I dashed to the engine room. The valve was open. I tried to start the engine again. Nothing. I called a nearby dredging barge on the VHF. No response.

Still, the momentum of the barge's 120,000 pound mass kept us moving forward. I steered to the center of the channel. Not wanting to be blown aground by the wind (which would be very difficult to unground into the wind), I stationed son Justin forward at the anchor windlass. I went to the stern as the wind gradually neutralized our headway. As our way slowly died, I threw over the aft emergency anchor. The aft anchor brought the barge firmly to a stop. I signaled Justin to drop the forward anchor. The two anchors grabbed immediately. We took up the excess line quickly in a race against the wind-induced sideslip. The barge strained at her lines, and held.

With our barge held securely off the shallow sand flats by our two anchors, I returned to the engine room and disconnected the fuel hose. I discovered a line, valve, and fuel filter solidly clogged with rust. A wire coat hanger became a handy deplugging tool. An hour later we were underway. The next day we installed a Separ fuel filter for extra protection. We also flushed the day tank sump weekly for a couple months until the loose rust was thoroughly flushed out. Each time I did so, I remembered the anchors with gratitude.

Whether carefully planned or in an emergency anchor splash, proper anchoring technique is an essential skill.

There are really two great joys in barging: when cruising, and when moored. Because Europe has some absolutely spectacular settings in which to moor one's home, the ability to secure your vessel comfortably in a wide variety of situations, whether tied to mooring buoys or rings in a city wall, secured to your own pins and land anchors on a pastoral rural bank, beached into a gravelly lake bank, or anchored serenely at sunset—all will enable you to enjoy those sites in safety.

I might add that if you are flying the American flag, it will give you a quiet sense of satisfaction as your calm professional barge handling answers the question implicit in the observant European gazes.

Chapter 5

LOCKS

This is the most important safety chapter in the book. If you read no other chapter, read this one.

The subject of this chapter remains alien to the experience of most Americans. I, for one, was so road oriented that when I thought commercial Renaissance I thought roads. Well, maybe not "roads" exactly, but their beginnings as ruts through the woods where peddlers traipsed with donkey and cart from one castle to another trading goods.

HISTORY

I was surprised to learn, then, that a major stimulus to the commercial Renaissance occurred when an Italian refined a Chinese idea on how to get a boat up the mountains and down the valleys in France. This is the same man who painted the Mona Lisa and designed an airplane and a way to get out of it--the parachute. Fortunately for European culture (and us), his design of a water elevator for boats--completed about the time Christopher Columbus discovered the "Indies"--had a more immediate practical reception than his air machines. Leonardo da Vinci's refinement of the lock, which Marco Polo had observed in the Orient, opened for the first time an avenue for cheap waterborne commerce. Now, huge loads could be delivered relatively easily over quite long distances. One barge could carry the loads of a hundred donkey carts. Furthermore, aboard the barge, all those loads could be pulled by one donkey.

Some bargers could afford donkeys and some could not. Some could only afford family, who tugged on the lines, thankful I am sure, when Leonardo's device came into sight to give them a rest.

Da Vinci's lock worked with amazing simplicity. It consisted of two sets of gates, which closed together at a slight angle like doors, "pointing" into the higher body of water. The force of the water kept the gates tightly closed when water levels differed. Once the water levels were equalized, they opened quite easily, pulled by leverage, gears, and wheels.

Once a gate opened, the barge would come in, close the gate behind it and either raise or lower the water in the lock, depending upon which way the barge was going. It was easy to raise or lower the water level. Little "windows" below the water level in the big gates were pulled open, allowing water in from the high side for traveling up in a lock, or out on the low side for going down in a lock, until the water level equalized. The far set of gates then opened and the barge departed on its new level. No pumps and gadgets. Just gates that opened and closed, and windows to let water in or out.

The sizes of locks vary tremendously. Still, one can traverse ancient locks that have been working the same way for nearly two hundred years. Cruising through Europe's canals is truly a transit through a veritable museum of locks.

TYPES

Europe's largest locks are on the larger rivers and canals of Germany, Holland, and Belgium. Some are longer than several football fields placed end to end and can accommodate huge two story barges filled with containerized cargo.

The locks on moderate sized rivers in these countries (plus France) are the easiest to use. They are always manned, operate by electric power, and, being so wide, are easy to enter.

The small locks in Holland, Belgium, and France are mainly sized to the so-called Napoleonic standard and can take but one barge or, on occasion, two smaller boats. They usually operate by hand, though some in France are automated.

By far the greatest number of locks are to be found in France. A quick look at a topographic map will tell you why. The flatlands of Holland and northern Belgium have such slight elevation changes they rarely require locks. France, on the other hand, contains hills, ranges, summits, and plateaus, all of which must be climbed and descended, and all by locks. The small locks also tend to be the oldest, many around 200 years old.

Incidentally, a Dutch or Flemish lock is called a "*sluis*", pronounced "slowz"; a French or Wallonian lock is an "*ecluse*", pronounced "A clews'"; and a German lock is a "*schleuse*".

LOCK PROCEDURES

Large locks (capable of holding more than one barge)....

Commercial barges enter first. All larger locks in Holland, Germany, and Belgium have VHF (Very High Frequency, used for marine radios) channels by which you can forewarn lockmasters of your arrival and they, in turn, can tell you when and where to moor within the lock.

Whenever possible, moor to port (assuming a right hand turning prop). Because of the torque effect, as discussed in chapter two, it is easier to stop and to depart with the port hull against the wall.

Approach the bollard inside the lock very slowly. An impatient lockmaster may hasten you into the lock, but once inside the gates, pick a mooring and slow down immediately. Get the barge under control.

Always secure the bowline first. The crew in the bow should look back at the skipper as the barge is slowing to confirm which lock bollard to use. A simple hand signal will communicate whether to put the mooring line around the next bollard or one further on. The skipper must retain control. Otherwise, confusion will result, with its consequent dangers.

To secure the bowline, the crew should have a boat hook ready in case it is needed to lift the line to the lock bollard. European boat hooks have both a metal point and a metal hook. They look a bit like a thumb pointing forward and the index finger curled aft. By resting the line between the point and the hook one can deposit it over the lock bollard quite professionally.

In a large lock, never put the loop end of the mooring line (picture it in your mind, now) over the lock bollard. Sooner or later, it will get stuck when you try to remove it and will either be way under water in a filling lock, or way up there in a descending lock. Instead, secure the loop end to a boat bollard, run the line around the lock bollard and back to the barge. That way you can always pull on one end and bring it free.

After the line is looped around the lock bollard, leave plenty of slack until the barge comes to a stop. Don't try to stop the barge with the line. You lose every time. The only result will be a crunch into the lock wall at best or jammed fingers or legs at worst. Let the skipper stop the barge with reverse engine. After the barge is stopped, take up the slack.

Once the bow is secured, it is fairly simple to maneuver the stern into place with the rudder hard over and the engine in idle forward.

Now you have a choice. If you have adequate crew, I recommend that you secure the stern line to a bollard, just as you did the bow. Then, unless you are in one of the few locks with floating bollards which rise with the water level, the crew will release the line from the lower bollard (if you are rising) and secure it to the next upper bollard. Of course, the reverse is true if you are descending. First do the bow, then the stern, then the bow, and so on, so at least one line secures the boat at all times.

If you are short on crew, you can do what many of the professional bargers do. They only use a bowline, but employ it as a "forespring". They secure it to a lock bollard about one third boat length aft of the bow. The bowline leads aft from the bow and points to the bollard at a fairly flat, though slightly raised, angle. Use the engine to slowly take up the slack. Once taut, leave the engine in idle forward with the rudder slightly off center so as to keep both bow and stern snug against the wall of the lock. As you rise (or descend), momentarily put the transmission in neutral to release the line tension as the crew places the bowline around the next lock bollard, and then slowly, carefully take up the tension once again. Either method will work. Try both and see what works best for you.

A few of the larger locks, especially in Belgium, have bollards only at the top. Normally a lockkeeper will place the mooring line over the bollard for you, since it is well beyond your reach. If you are rising, of course, you may use the loop end of the line since there is no danger of it becoming stuck--you will rise to its level. When going down, however, unless you know the lockkeeper assistant will release the line for you, keep the loop end on the boat so you can retrieve the line when you are at the bottom of the lock.

Unless directed otherwise by the lockmaster, don't moor too far forward in the lock or too near the stern of a large barge. Going too far forward, especially in a rising lock, may subject your boat to tremendous currents from the gate valves as they let the water rush in from the high side. Mooring too near the stern of a large barge means its skipper must be very careful when leaving to avoid blasting you with prop wash.

Finally, if commercial barges leave before you do, remain moored until their wash will no longer bounce you off the walls. Then, after you cast off and clear the wall, give her a little extra steam to push through the after currents.

Small locks

Enter very slowly. Very, very slowly. Neither stone nor steel has much give. Approaches to your first small locks will be with the gearshift in neutral. If your barge is almost as wide as the lock (lock width is 5 meters, or about 16 feet) you will find that you bump the lock entrance and walls more than you want. As you gain confidence, try another, less bouncy tactic. Slow down in neutral on the approach; then, ten to twenty feet before the lock, slip the transmission back into idle forward. You enter just a hair faster, but have better control over the barge. The steering will be much more responsive for those last minute fine tune adjustments.

One other hint. Remember when you first learned to drive a car?

You erred by looking at the white line directly in front of the car instead of fixing your gaze down the road a bit. The same principle applies to entering locks. Line up the centerline of the barge with the centerline of the lock. It is easy to spot the centerline at the far end of the lock--it's where the two gates meet. The near entrance is more difficult. Often there is a bridge above the gates and sometimes there is a vertical line painted on the bridge that marks the centerline of the lock. Your barge may also have a flagstaff for the courtesy flags mounted amidship.

I also like to glue a piece of white paper cut as an inverted narrow V, or arrow, on my windshield at eye level. All these aids provide "gunsights" that you can line up to bring the barge straight in. If there is no such bridge or line or mast or arrow--just imagine them. I stand directly in the center of the barge and sight straight along my white paper "sight" to the flagstaff and the point of the bow. I can aim her like sighting a rifle. Ideally, line up all points on a straight sharpshooter line: yourself and the arrow on the centerline of the barge, the flagstaff, the point of the bow, the center of the lock entrance, and the center of the far end of the lock.

It may be helpful to imagine your barge is an airplane and the lock is the runway. With an airplane, the angle of approach makes all the difference. The approach needs to be absolutely straight. So the pilot draws an invisible line in the sky and flies the airplane right along it until he settles the aircraft right over the white line that marks the center of the runway. As the barge pilot, position your barge for a straight approach.

One way to determine whether or not your approach is straight I call the "lock wall" method. As I approach, I see how much of the right wall I can see compared to the left wall. If one is fat and the other slim, I'm off to one side. I correct until the amount of lock wall on the right and left are equal. Can you see that?

Now, very important, alternate your gaze between the imaginary centerline and the sides of the lock. This will be more effective than concentrating solely on the potential points of impact at the entrance. Put the center of the barge (the middle fore and aft as well as amidships--the point where a giant finger would balance the barge in the air) right along the imaginary centerline extension of the lock--just like landing the airplane. It does not matter so much if the bow is off the line or even if the stern is. Put the center of the boat on the line. You have time to correct for the bow to enter properly after the barge center is directly on the line.

So the main thing is a straight approach, using the aircraft approach method and the "lock wall" method. Then fine-tune with the gunsights.

Once the bow pokes into the lock, ease the transmission into neutral, then ease into reverse. This means reverse torque. So swing the wheel as you hit reverse, anticipating the reverse torque so you stop straight. Look aft as the stern comes in to see if it will hit the walls.

These small locks will normally have bollards (or angled mooring rods) only at the top of the lock. If in a rising lock, your crew will need to put the loop end of the mooring line on the tip of the boat hook and stretch to slip it over the bollard or bent rod. An alternate method is to keep the loop end in one hand and fling a coiled length of line cowboy-like over the bollard. Use whatever works best for you.

In many of the smaller locks, it is sufficient to secure only the bowline. In others, however, there is such turbulent water action from the gate "windows" being opened that it is advisable to secure the barge both fore and aft. When in doubt, secure both. Once again, you may use the bowline led aft but kept under tension as described in the procedures for big locks above.

In the smaller locks, when rising, the rush of incoming water from the gate valves creates a peculiar phenomenon. One would think--since the water is coming through valves in the lock gates forward of the barge--that the barge would be shoved aft by the torrent of water coming in. And that does occur, at first. Soon, however, the barge starts surging forward. Why? The incoming water shoots under the boat, hits the aft gates and bounces up and forward, carrying the barge forward with it. Keep this phenomenon in mind when you tie off so your barge doesn't crash into the forward gates.

Make sure the crew and any guests are well instructed on their duties.

My father was visiting us on the barge, having flown in the day before from California. He assisted ably on several locks and I assumed he had the procedure down pretty well. He offered to handle the bowline by himself as we entered the next lock. When I saw him loop the bollard, I went below to, well, check out the plumbing. The next thing I heard was shouting, a thump, a roar of the engine, and a crash!

Here is what happened. Dad assumed that once we were stopped in the lock, his job was finished. He dropped his end of the bowline on the deck--big mistake. The aft gates closed and the lockkeeper opened the gate valves forward, letting the upper level canal water rush into the lock. First we drifted aft, then our 120,000 pound barge surged forward with the bounce back current. The lockkeeper yelled in French. Dad yelled in English. Our 14 year-old son Justin, by then a veteran of three countries and about 250 locks, sized up the situation from his lockkeeper-helping position where he had been cranking lock gates. He leaped onto the barge (thump!), shoved the gearshift into reverse and blew out the carbon deposits in the cylinders. His action slowed us a lot, almost enough to prevent the gentle crash into the forward lock gates.

Fortunately, the only damage was a dismayed lockkeeper, a quaking father, and a more careful skipper. After a little filing and some paint, I challenge anyone to find the point of impact on our bow. But it was a lesson well learned and an example of how things can go wrong in a hurry.

When entering a descending (full) lock, once again do not put the loop end of the line over the bollard or bent rod, because you will have difficulty extracting it when you are at the bottom of the lock.

Water turbulence in a descending lock is negligible compared to an ascending lock.

As you leave a lock, be aware of torque. Accelerate slowly and watch the stern as you leave to avoid scraping against the lock walls.

PRECAUTIONS FOR ALL LOCKS!!!

Please read this next section twice. Then go back and read it again. Then read it to your crew. Then recite it as you lie in bed tonight. This addresses what is probably the most dangerous part of cruising.

More accidents happen inside locks than anywhere else. But accidents can be prevented by strict--and I mean **strict**--attention to a few simple rules.

1. **Keep feet and legs inside the barge and off the lock walls at all times!** The barge is far too heavy to stop by hand. It will only crush, and steel is much more fixable than bone. If you see a crash coming, other than placing a tough fender at the point of impact, let it happen. Keep feet, hands, and legs away. Believe it or not, my dear father was trying to push the barge away from those forward gates with his hands as we charged into them!

2. **Never, never, never step inside a mooring line coil on deck!** Always coil lines carefully after use. Always. Either feed lines into a coil on the deck (strongly recommended) or loop it with your hands. If looping it in your hands, add a half twist at the end of each loop so it hangs in a circle instead of a figure eight twisted loop. Then place the coiled line close to the centerline of the barge, **away** from the bollard so that there is plenty of room for the crew to stand without placing a foot inside the coil. We like to take it one step further and keep the mooring lines in flat coiled mats that look like giant drink coasters. More nautical, cleaner looking, and certainly safer. Normally you would have one coil per bollard (four total), all lying near the centerline.

When descending in a lock (now visualize this carefully) the crew must feed out line as the barge descends with the water level. Makes sense, right? If your crew should get the line coiled around their foot or leg and should the line with leg be drawn irrevocably by the lowering water into the boat bollard.... You can see what will happen. And it does, every year. A German lady showed us the multiple scars on her leg when she did it. She required several surgeries to save her multi-fractured leg. My wife Marlene and ten year old son Danny had it happen momentarily, and only by quick action did each unwrap the line from their leg before it became taut. Drill, drill, drill your crew! Then drill some more!

3. **When in a descending lock, NEVER tie off the lines on the boat!** Lines must always be able to run free. Never tie off (secure) the line to the boat bollard when you expect to descend. In fact, you may wish to make a rule to never tie off in a lock, period. The consequences in a descending lock are obvious--the water goes down but the boat does not, still tied to the bollard.

We were the last boat to enter a large Dutch lock on the Maas. There must have been twenty boats lined up along both lock walls and the only place left for our barge was in the middle of the pack, with boats on both sides. We were by far the largest craft in the lock and all the natives were interested in watching the American with the big boat thread the needle among these fiberglass boats. We entered without incident and tied carefully to the largest powerboat we could find. The gates closed behind us. The warning siren sounded, telling all boaters that the water was about to be released, lowering us all to the new level. We began to descend. Suddenly, voices cried out beside us. A smaller powerboat to our right tilted wildly, its mooring lines still tied to the top of the lock wall. Evidently, the crew, while waiting for all the boats to enter the lock, had tied off and then had become so engrossed in observing us they forgot to untie their lines. Now, the boat was nearly completely on its side, hanging from the wall, as the last of the crew, a lady, clambered out of the cabin and up the side of the boat, pulling herself up the mooring lines like a mountain climber to the top of the lock where hands reached down to pull her to safety.

A knife appeared from nowhere and quickly sliced both mooring lines. With the sickening screech of fiberglass against concrete the powerboat splashed back into the water. Fortunately, although the lady's leg was scraped and bleeding, there were no serious injuries. This story has a simple moral: **never** tie off the lines when the water is going down.

4. **When in a descending lock, lead the mooring line from the lock bollard under one ear of the boat bollard, then, for friction, loop it kitty-corner halfway around the next bollard**. Other than placing the loop end over a boat bollard, do **not** take a full 360 degree wrap around **any** bollard. The crew should ease the line as the boat descends, but there should be no opportunity for the line to

proper lines for descending

catch on itself or develop an overwrap which would cause the line to bind on the boat bollard and hang up the boat.

Permit another illustration. This occurred in a smaller lock, the standard Napoleonic size in France, in an automated section as we descended through a long series, having just emerged from a tunnel at the summit. From time to time we would see the little blue vans of the "Service de Navigation" which monitored the canals and locks as they drove down the canalside towpaths en route to a lock needing some work. As we entered this particular lock, a little blue van stopped; the man took his lunch break, breaking out a baguette and wine. We went through the locking sequence, lifting the blue rod inside the lock wall (explained in more detail later) to activate the closure of the gates behind us and the subsequent lowering of the water level in the lock. Our second son Danny had correctly placed the loop end of the mooring line around a boat bollard on the bow, then led the line over the lock bollard and back to the other boat bollard (whenever there is one boat bollard, there is normally a second beside it). He sat on the coachroof ready to feed the line as we descended. So far, so good.

The gates closed behind us and a few seconds later the "windows" in the lock gates forward opened mechanically. They released lock water and initiated our descent. Everything seemed normal as I sat in the pilothouse, observing. The technician on lunch break munched away in his van. As the boat slowly went down with the water level in the lock, I noticed Danny stare intently at the bollards, then quickly jump to his feet as he tried to unwrap the line from around a boat bollard. Without even seeing the line, I knew instantly what was happening. His line was snagged in a bind on the boat bollard. He had taken an extra wrap around the bollard and friction caused it to bind on itself. The line could not feed and the boat could not descend. I ran forward. Taking the line from him, I saw that tension was now squeezing the line between the loop and the steel ears of the bollard. As the descending barge increased the grip of the bind, it became ever more difficult to release. I took a quick reverse wrap against the grain and gave the strongest yank I could, trying to jerk the line out from under the ear. It wouldn't give. I yanked again. No good. Now the barge started to list, as the water level dropped every part of the barge except the bow ever lower. I yelled at Justin to lift the red emergency rod as I ran back to the cabin for the knife to cut the line. Three things then happened simultaneously. Justin pulled up the red emergency rod which immediately closed the "windows" and prevented any further lowering of the water level in the lock; the man in the little blue van saw what was happening and ran to the control house; and I arrived at the bow with the knife, ready to slice the line and free the barge.

I paused with my arm uplifted, ready to come down with the knife--had the boat stopped descending? Yes it had. Whew! However, we still could not release the line and I concluded I would have to cut it. It was already straining heavily, tiny strands popping under the stress. The Frenchman, sensing my predicament, signaled for me to not to cut the line. He entered the control house and refilled the lock, raising the boat until the tension on the line eased and we were able to release it.

Danny learned a lesson I am sure he will never forget and I used the experience to illustrate to the rest of the family to never, never, never take a full wrap around the bollard in a descending lock.

LOCKS AND CRUISE PLANNING

Want to know how far you might cruise today? How many locks are there? In Holland, count the kilometers to your destination; in France, count the locks. In that country, locks, rather than distance frequently will dictate your progress. Generally, figure 20 minutes per lock. We have done better and we have done a lot worse, especially when we have to wait for the lock to clear (which is infrequent). France's automatic locks are the fastest, while the hand operated locks depend on the speed of the hands operating it. Generally, a ten to fifteen lock day is a pretty heavy day. Otherwise the cruise gets too much like work and you don't have time to enjoy what cruising is all about.

FRENCH LOCKS

The canal locks of France, though nearly uniform in size, employ a variety of methods to open and close their gates. Some, along the Burgundy canal in central France, use a large wheel that looks like the steering wheel on an old ship. The wheel turns a chain wrapped around its hub which in turn rotates a gear, pulling a bar attached to the gate. Also along the Burgundy canal is another system that uses long horizontal steel poles which the lockkeeper pushes. These long poles, through interconnected levers which provide mechanical advantage, are attached to the gate. By far the most common system, however, is a simple gearbox fixed at waist height beside the lock gate. The lockkeeper (at one gate, you at the opposite gate), inserts a wrench-like handle and turns the gear box protrusion which rotates a large gear, like one might imagine in a giant clock. The teeth on the gear interleave into those on a steel beam attached to the gate. A little arm exercise opens the lock gate.

To save manpower costs, France has launched a lock automation program. Yet it seems each series of locks uses a different type of equipment. I will describe some of the more common types of automatic locks here, but there are bound to be additional types you may encounter among the thousands of locks in France.

We work through a Napoleonic sized lock in France.

The most common automatic lock we encountered uses an electric eye to detect the approaching barge. The eye is located about 100 yards before the lock along the right hand bank and is housed in a gray bulb about the size of a small volleyball. This bulbous housing sits atop a skinny pipe structure about six feet tall which from a distance appears to be some sort of space alien basketball star. Pass slowly in front of this eye and it will activate the lock for you. Small boats and fiberglass boats have difficulty getting noticed by this detector, and sometimes have to go extremely slowly by it. Other times they have to disembark a crewmember with a cast iron pan to hold in front of the round gray eye for about ten seconds.

Some of the automatic locks, instead of having the gray alien-looking electric eye on the approach, have a rubber tube about one inch in diameter and eight feet long, suspended from a wire over the canal. The idea is to grab hold of the tube as you pass under it and twist it 1/4 turn either left or right. This, like the electric eye, alerts the lock to your approach.

Red and green stoplights on the lock wall next to the gate inform the approaching skipper what the lock is doing to prepare for his arrival. Red means the lock either doesn't know the barge exists or there is a barge from the other side that is entering or is already in the lock. When both red and green lights glow at the same time (which, if the lock is available, should occur within about 15 seconds of activating the electric eye) it means the lock recognizes the approaching barge and is preparing for its entrance. One of two things will now happen. If the water level in the lock is the same as the barge's, the doors will open. Once the gates are fully open, the green light only will glow. If, however, the gates don't immediately open, the lock will either empty itself or fill itself to accommodate the barge. There are a few cautions here.

If you are descending through a series of locks, the locks will have to be full before you can enter (so you can descend the water staircase). If it is empty when you alert the electric eye, it must of course fill itself before it can open its gates and let you in. Guess where the filling water comes from? From where you are. A lock is larger than a swimming pool. That is a lot of water and the fill happens fast. Whoosh! You will feel the barge being drawn toward the lock, even though you are perfectly stopped, just like a bath tub toy is drawn to the drain when the plug is pulled. If the barge is too close to the lock you will have to hit reverse, back away and deal with the effects of torque as you try to back up straight. Gist of the story--if the lock must fill, stop far enough from the lock so as not to be sucked into the gate (but close enough to have tripped the electric eye, of course).

What if you are in ascending locks, gradually climbing through the countryside? In some cases you will need to wait while the lock empties. You will see the rush of water gurgle up at the base of the lock gates as it disgorges. The lock will empty, the gates will open, and you will be tempted to rush in. My advice--don't be in a hurry; wait awhile. The sudden discharge of water through the gate valves sets off a swirling sequence of currents that bounces off the canal banks and is almost impossible to navigate without getting the barge angled somehow, just at a time when you are trying to make a very, very straight approach to avoid scraping the hull sides on the lock's masonry. Let the currents subside. A couple minutes of patience will pay off in easier entry.

As you think about the effect of water currents on one's entry into locks, let me alert you to one other concern. Many French canals are constructed along former stream beds and carry a streamflow which can be particularly pronounced in the spring and after a heavy rainfall. Since the lock acts pretty much like a dam, many locks have a bypass tube that runs underground from the desired water level above the lock to the water level below the lock. The problem occurs on the low side of the lock. The water streams from the tube, accelerated by the approximate eight foot drop in water level, and often enters the canal beside the lower lock gate. It shoots a stream of water across your route of entry. This current will of course move you sideways, ruining your careful entry into the lock. Hence, you must adjust your approach to compensate for the sideways drift caused by the tube current. The degree of adjustment is an art, refined by practice. You will gain immense satisfaction as you execute a delicate straight non-side-scraping entry into the lock after correctly anticipating the various effects of wind and water currents.

Inside the automatic lock, you will find that a blue rod and a red rod extend down an indent in the side wall of the lock (sometimes the blue one is green). The red rod is only for emergencies. Lifting it stops all lock operations and summons a lockkeeper. Once you have secured the barge, lift the blue rod for five seconds, or until the gates begin to close. The lock will now go through a programmed sequence: the gates behind you close, the water level changes, and the gates on the far side of the lock open for your exit. An electric eye detects your departure.

Some locks have a variation. They have a steel bar with a curved end which sticks out about three feet into the lock just above water level near the gate. As you enter, you must depress the bar against the wall of the lock for five seconds, either with your passing hull or with a boat hook. It is a safety feature designed to assure that you are inside the lock before the gates close. Similarly, upon departure you must depress an exit bar to program the lock to prepare for the next barge.

A guest hoists a beer on a warm October day to a lockeeper, who assists us because the automatic mechanisms fail. The right rod is red, lifted in emergencies. The left rod is blue and is lifted for a few seconds to activate the lock functions.

We encountered a variant we call the garage door opener. This replaces the function of the metal bar and the electric eye upon exit. Here is how it works: as you enter the lock (after the gates have been opened by the gray alien, the twisted tube, the lockmaster, or by an electronic sequence activated by your departure from the previous lock) you depress the button on the little brown plastic garage door opener as you aim it at an amber light fixture situated by the lock gate. As soon as the electric beam hits the amber fixture it lights up, just as an American garage door opener turns on a garage light. The amber light also indicates the lock is ready to accept your commands via the blue rod. Similarly, when you leave, "shoot" the amber fixture near the opposite gate to let the lock know you are leaving. After a minute or so, the gates will close behind you and in many cases, the next lock will be electronically notified of your approach.

In our experience, these automatic locks work very well in theory and most often in practice. The problem comes with two way traffic. The locks handle the sequence of your locking through just fine until you meet a barge from the opposite direction. The computer occasionally gets confused as to who is going what direction. The best way to avoid confusion is to let the oncoming barge pass by before you trip the gray alien or twist the rubber tube, provided there is one. Wait far enough back from the lock, allow the barge to pass and the lock to close, and then begin your sequence. Sometimes, of course, you will be already through the approach sensors before you see the oncoming barge and there is nothing to do but hope it works well. At other times, the computer will have figured things out and hold the gates open for you after the oncoming barge has exited.

If nothing works, many locks have an emergency phone to summon a lockkeeper. Others permit VHF radio contact when there is difficulty.

France can be justly proud of her canal and lock system but the automated portion certainly lacks the uniformity that Napoleon idealized. The inclined plane, however, is one piece of non-uniformity Napoleon would have been proud of, I think. He liked innovation and this is certainly innovative. Located along what is   nearly a cliff as one approaches the quaint village of Lutzelbourg from the east en route to Strasbourg, this unique lock uses what may be called a "bathtub". The boats float in the bathtub as it slips down the slide sideways, controlled by cables and counterweights. The inclined plane is clearly the most sophisticated and delightful of all locks to be found on any of Europe's waterways, from small canals to large rivers.

On the opposite end of the scale are the round, or egg-shaped locks. Whoever designed these atrocities doubtless received the guillotine. The inventor, I'm sure, detested straight corners. Witness the rounded sides and the rounded bottoms--it's like entering a giant oval swimming pool with slanting sides for the kids. Or a giant clam shell. Of course, if you enter from the low end, the sides are slimy and slippery so you must disembark a crewmember by a slick stairway inlaid in the sloped bottom to secure the lines. And if you enter from the high side, the crew must pole your barge off the same sloping bottom so you don't get hung up as the water drains. Fortunately, there are mercifully few of these abominations.

The larger rivers, notably the Meuse, Seine, Moselle, Oise, and Rhone have quite large locks, often located in pairs to handle two way traffic. They can hold several large barges plus smaller craft like yours slipped in to the small spaces, though in our experience there is seldom a lack of space in these large locks. The traffic light system works the same on these as it does on the smaller automated single barge locks.

Unlike most other countries, who operate on a first come, first served basis, France gives priority to commercial barges. I suggest that you give priority to commercial barges in any case. They have a lot more at stake in making time, probably, than you and I.

Regardless of the country, it is always good boatsmanship to allow the largest, most difficult to handle craft into the lock first, and then fill in with smaller, more maneuverable craft.

Overall, as a guest in someone else's country, the best advice I can give is not to try to press your "rights". Be cordial and respectful, and more than likely it will be returned ten-fold. It certainly was for us.

Historically, a lockkeeper and his family serviced one lock. Their often quaint lockhouses were situated beside the lock. In some sections, especially those with longer stretches between locks, lockkeepers still operate in the traditional manner. They emerge from their home as you approach to prepare the lock for your entry. After you leave, the lockkeeper sometimes will call ahead to the next lockhouse and announce your approach. Other times your appearance seems a total surprise and a gentle toot on the horn is needed to rouse the lockkeeper.

Some lockhouses are not occupied by lockkeepers at all but by renters. Canal rumor told us these houses could be rented from the French government for $100 per year. However, a lockkeeper gave us the distinct impression the lockhouses were the personal fiefdom of the chief of the canal district to dispense as he wished. If you were on his good side, he said, you could live there for free. Otherwise you may have to pay rent or perhaps not be considered at all. Unfortunately, many of these lockhouses now stand vacant, doors blocked, windows boarded, orchards unpruned--orchards that still provide apples, pears, and walnuts for the gleaning barger. Still others, sadly, are being demolished.

Along many sections of canal, you will be assigned a lockkeeper during your transit. He will meet you at the first lock and zip ahead on his little moped along the towpath to prepare the next lock for you. Some will accompany you from lock to lock, others for a half day or so. They seldom know English but even if you don't know French, you can often manage to communicate if you are creative. These folk come in a wide variety of personalities, some of whom will be sparklingly hospitable and others who will grunt along. Please don't allow your rejected courtesies to the latter spoil a possible friendship with the former.

The moped lockkeepers are mainly men, whereas frequently the residential lockkeepers are women, in which case I suspect the lockkeeping supplements family income as she tends locks and he earns another living. Although the French government seems to be cutting back on canal staff, a government publication stated it was being accomplished by attrition rather than by laying anyone off. It seems an attractive vocation. One new lockkeeping family along the Burgundy canal told us that they had to compete with 200 others for one opening. Civil service tests determined his selection, according to his Scottish-born wife.

> Although previously there had been no charge for recreational craft to use the French locks, a fee was introduced in 1993. It is based on the size of the vessel and may be purchased for one week at a time, 45 days, or for the entire year. Permits are available from *Librairie VNF*, 2 bd de Latour-Maubourg, 75343 Paris, Cedex 07, France, FAX 011-33-1-47-05-81-38. Provide name and address, name of boat, overall length and beam, square meters (length x beam), registration number or hull number, type of permit required, and a stamped addressed envelope. Post the permit on the starboard side of the pilothouse.

Courtesies in French Locks

Each vocation has particular courtesies and customs that surround it, and one with the historic traditions of lockkeeping certainly is no exception. The golden rule is to be friendly and helpful whenever you can. We always tried to avoid the perception of the "prima donna American" who throws money around and expects all foreigners to do his bidding. Beyond that, however, there are certain "niceties" to observe.

It is appropriate that someone from the barge open one of the exit gates while the lockkeeper opens the other. That is about all you can do to assist unless you have an enterprising crew like our young boys who sometimes, for exercise, ran ahead of the barge to help open the gates for our entry.

The lockkeeper will want to take a lunch break, normally precisely at noon, and normally for an hour. Violating one's lunch hour borders on sacrilege in Europe, one of the lifestyle elements that contrasts with the American experience. When you run automatic locks, of course, you can set your own schedule. But otherwise a 12:01 arrival at a lock means you may relax until 1:00 PM (1300 hours to them, since Europe uses a 24 hour clock). If you are accompanied by a moped lockkeeper, he will often let you spend the lunch hour in the lock, which saves you from having to tie to the canal bank. If you have a resident lockkeeper, however, it occasionally seems a violation of canal custom to spend the noon hour inside his lock. On the other hand, we had some residential lockkeepers work into their noon hour to get us out of their locks and on our way, provided of course that we entered his lock decently before noon.

It is a good idea to let the lockkeeper know when you plan to stop for the night, so he can plan his schedule as well as that of the lockkeeper he will hand you off to. They will then want to know what time you plan to leave in the morning. Good manners says to keep that schedule, of course, so you don't keep him waiting. If the language is so baffling that you and the lockkeeper cannot communicate time, use the idea of an English barging acquaintance. He drew a dozen clock faces on a sheet of paper, each with hands set an hour apart. He then pointed to the clock face that showed his time of departure the next morning.

Sometimes the lockkeeper will do seemingly inexplicable things that, unless you speak quite good French, baffle you. Be understanding. You will often see the reason later. Perhaps a large barge is coming the other way and the lockkeeper wants to position you in the best place to meet the barge. Other times there may be a mechanical problem with the next lock or the lock system needs to adjust their staffing due to different boats going different directions on differing schedules. Patience is the key word.

Tipping the lockkeeper is a matter of individual choice. We varied the tip, when we felt one was appropriate, to the amount of effort and the hospitality of the lockkeeper. We did not tip the one-time "residential lockkeepers" but usually tipped a moped lockkeeper, especially if he was friendly and did at least 4 locks with us. We avoided tipping with cash because it seems impersonal and contributes to the "rich foreigner" syndrome. We preferred to give a token of some meaning, though it need not cost much. Some of the gifts we used were chocolate bars or cookies. We discovered many lockkeepers like American whiskey in the little single serving bottles. Those that smoke appreciate a pack of American cigarettes or a good cigar. On a hot day, a bottle of beer is appreciated but we learned to avoid giving American wine or beer. Europeans are justly proud of their wines and beers and some may misinterpret your gift as a bit of a national insult.

> I recall one mistake we made. It was a hot day in central France and we thought our sweaty French lockkeeper, having accompanied us for about ten locks, might like a cool Coors. I'll never forget the look on his face at his first taste. He would take a swig and then stare at the can as if trying to figure how such a taste could come from such a can. (As you may know, European beers are more full-bodied than ours, which I suspect tastes like watered down pop to them). After this sequence of swigs and stares, with a long pull he finally drained the can. His face appeared strained from the effort. It reminded me of the look we would get as one of our boys' guests at dinner sampled an unfamiliar vegetable. I wondered if the only reason he finished the Coors was to avoid insulting us. Once the can was empty, he tossed it over his shoulder into the canal below the lock. We were shocked but wiser.

As a general rule, we found the Europeans to be profoundly generous and gracious hosts. A Belgian doctor we moored with in Brugge, Belgium showered us with Belgian chocolates and wine; a German sailor pressed us with bottles of German white wine, fine cigars, chocolates for the kids, and delicate slices of his home-cured leg of smoked pork, after but a day's acquaintance; a French barger worked with me a good part of a day unplugging a clogged head outlet (now that's hospitality!); and the Dutch gave us flowers, chocolate and "*Jonge Jenever*".

How often we wished we had more to give in return! We yearned for some small, unique American gift that we could offer. The tokens we managed, like Blue Diamond "smokehouse" almonds from my father's California orchards, were soon gone. You will find your trip enriched by being able to return the fine hospitality of these gracious people. Select something suitable before your journey and pack lots of it. Your generosity will leave a trail of good will toward you in particular and toward

Americans in general that cannot be matched by any amount of State Department diplomacy.

DUTCH LOCKS

Like all locks, the Dutch locks reflect the size of their waterways. Theirs are the most diverse waterways on the continent, from the widest of rivers to the tiniest of canals. Although the great rivers, particularly the magnificent spreading Rhine (called the Waal in Holland), have no locks, a series of very large commercial arterials which link these rivers do. These locks are designed to accommodate the largest of the river giants and are easy to use.

One of the fascinating aspects of cruising Holland, however, is her spider web of tiny canals that meander through the pastoral countryside. Using the chart, check the dimensions of the locks on these little canals to make sure you will fit. The tightest fitting lock we squeezed into on our 16 month, 5,000 kilometer, 915 lock cruise was in Holland. Ironically, it was the first lock as we left on our cruise, and the last when we finished. It was a bit easier the second time around.

Compared to hilly France, however, flat Holland has very few locks. Locking is a way of life in France, with locks sometimes every quarter mile or so, whereas a lock in Holland is a pleasant surprise. We transited more locks in one day in France (31 plus a tunnel, our record) than we did in Holland in two months of cruising!

Each Dutch lock has a VHF radio so you can talk to the "*sluismeester*", as he is called in the Netherlands. Although the Dutch are among the best English speakers on the continent, few of the lockkeepers speak English. Even though I speak a little Dutch, radio Dutch is about as understandable as radio English, which is one of the reasons why it is easier and probably just as fast to simply go in when the gates open for you rather than mess with the radio.

Dutch locks are modern and mechanized and easy to use. Since Holland is so flat, the water level differences are often minuscule. I remember how excited I became when early in our cruise, I found a three foot drop on the other side of the lock. I called out the family, took pictures, got just the right angles on the video camera, all to document this exciting event! On other occasions in Holland we would be surprised after we had secured the boat inside the lock to find the gates opening--we couldn't tell if we had gone up or down. The relatively minor changes in water levels and their convenient size are among the reasons that working the locks of Holland is easier than anywhere else in Europe.

That doesn't mean there aren't exceptions. The lock just south of the border town of Maastricht in southern Holland on the Maas River is one of the deepest in all of Europe. We literally dropped into the Netherlands--about 60 feet! And we found one of the most quaint and beautiful antitheses of modern, mechanized locks as we entered the wonderful little village of Makkum from the Ijsselmeer. The lockkeeper operates by hand the locks and bridges made in a wondrous wrought iron style of yesteryear.

Tipping on Dutch locks is the exception, only appropriate in the rare instance when the lock is operated by hand. Watch for signs, because the Dutch will often not leave these things to chance, and may well post the amount.

As far as other courtesies are concerned, the Dutch pretty much take care of everything for you in the lock, so there really is not a lot you can do to help. Though you may wish to help in the rare situation where there may be such an opportunity, be sure to ask first, since the self-sufficient Dutch quite like to complete their job the way they are taught.

All the locks on the commercial arterial canals are large enough to accommodate the big barges and still have plenty of room for you too. Unlike France, where commercial barges have priority at locks, Holland is first-come, first-served. Nevertheless, courtesy as well as boatsmanship dictate prudence: let the larger, commercial barges enter a lock first. It is somewhat similar to trucks and the American freeway. We can't go wrong promoting good relations between ourselves and the professionals. The more respectful we are toward the professional bargers, the more we will encourage their professionalism, engendering an atmosphere of courtesy and helpfulness on the waterways that benefits everyone.

On the whole, we found the commercial skippers conduct themselves to the highest standards. There will always be the occasional aberrant jerk, however, and you just need to swallow hard and count to ten in the language of your choice.

Other courtesies are pretty much standard. The only one worth emphasizing is relevant during late June to mid-August each year. That is when the school children are out and the Dutch take to their boats like ducks to water. You may feel like you are part of an aquatic multitude of lemmings migrating en masse down the canals. As you approach locks remember it is definitely considered aggressive and inconsiderate to try to pass as other boats slow down on the approach (though some natives are guilty). Wait your turn and hold your place.

Some of the locks of Holland may be closed on Sundays, particularly in the off season, so be sure to check the Dutch Boating Almanac or ask someone before planning a Sunday cruise.

BELGIAN LOCKS

Belgium is a charmingly oxymoronic country. Flemish in the north and Wallonian in the south, it is a linguistically, culturally, religiously, ethnically, and topographically divided country. The land of the Flemish (Flanders) is low and flat while that of the Wallonians is hilly, rising toward the French plateaus to the south.

The Flemish closely resemble their Dutch neighbors to the north (though many Flems will deny it with vehemence) in attitudes and language, as well they might, since history put them in the same country until a little over a hundred years ago. In fact, Belgium is a younger nation than the United States.

As the Flems in the north are related to the Dutch, so the Wallonians in the south are closely tied to the French. Wallonia is nearly as culturally and linguistically ethnocentric as France itself. Whereas many Flems speak English, the Wallonians, though trained in English in school, rarely will speak it. This is a fascinating country whose cultural domestic differences are reflected in their locks.

It should not come as a surprise to find differences between locking through Flanders and locking through Wallonia. For one thing, to learn about locks in Flanders one can reread the section above on Dutch locks and likewise, the section on French locks will largely apply to Wallonia. But there are a few exceptions. For example, Belgium once was a solid part of the French empire (more solid than the independent-minded provinces of what is now Holland) and Napoleon's edicts on canal and lock sizes were followed in Flanders more closely than in Holland.

The Meuse River, which originates in France and winds through eastern Belgium before becoming Holland's Maas River, has large locks that accommodate huge craft. This is Belgium's big river and has the country's big locks, save for those leading to the industrial areas of Antwerp, Brussels, and Gent from the Schelde Estuary along the Dutch-Belgian border. The rest of the country has mainly French type locks along French sized canals.

Once again there are exceptions, especially at the gigantic inclined plane of Roncieres, south of Brussels, which replaces some 19 conventional locks. It is larger than its French counterpart, and while not so steep, is considerably longer. The bathtub is oriented lengthwise instead of sideways as its glides up and down the angled plane. It is a most impressive affair.

Mechanization is the other difference which contrasts the Belgian with the French locks. Almost all the Belgian locks are mechanically powered, a bit larger, and handled by a large staff.

In 1990, it cost the equivalent of one dollar to use all of Belgium's locks, though we had to pay it in segments. Upon entering the country, our barge was entered into the computer, our entire route pre-logged, and the Belgian franc equivalent of our dollar extracted for most of our route through the country. The computer hummed and spat out a computerized sheet which I then had to take to nearly every lockkeeper for him to log and stamp. Finally, I had to turn the sheet in to the last lock or the border Douane (Customs) upon my departure from Belgium. It seemed to us rather silly to run around with this computer sheet to a uniformed bureaucrat whose only job, it appeared, was to log and stamp the papers of passing barges.

In 1991, Flanders (alone, not Wallonia) enacted a lock use fee for all its locks except those along the Meuse, amounting to the equivalent of $60 to $100, depending upon the size of the vessel. The effect, of course, will discourage nautical tourism of Flanders and put traffic bound to and from Holland and France onto the Meuse at least until they reach Wallonia.

What will happen in the future as a result of the volatile politics of a divided Belgium is anyone's guess. Adding to the uncertainty is the impact of "no border stops" throughout the 12 nation European Community. Lock paperwork procedures in Belgium—and elsewhere—could well change.

If you are in Holland, the latest information on Belgian locks will be available from the Dutch. They will know what is going on. And if you are in France, heading toward Belgium—well, the best idea is still to check with the Dutch. (For more, see Chapter 7, *Rivers and Canals*).

As far as Belgian courtesies are concerned, use your judgment depending on the situation, since you are sometime French, sometime Dutch. Generally, we didn't tip the mechanized lockkeepers, although, with their excess staff, they sometimes have a fellow available to catch your line and loop it around the lock bollard when you enter a deep lock from the low end.

Like Holland, boats are officially first come, first served.

GERMAN LOCKS

Except for those of the beautiful River Lahn, most of Germany's locks are of the large industrial type. The bigger the river, the bigger the barges and the bigger the locks. They function much like the large locks of Holland.

German locks are normally open every day of the week, though they sometimes close for selected holidays. Because German holidays are different than ours, you are well-advised to check in advance (as is true for all countries of Europe).

Our experience with German locks along the Rhine (the Rhine's only locks are south of Baden-Baden in the Black Forest), the Neckar, and the Mosel (same river as Moselle in France) is that the locks are so large as to render first-come, first served meaningless. Go with the big boys, but carefully.

Our only charge for locks in Germany was on the Mosel. But the fees only apply on the large locks (they have little ones for sport boats on that river), and only if there are no commercial barges in the lock with you. If you want to go alone, you may, but you pay--in 1991, about 10DM ($6) per lock for our 20 meter barge. The solution is simple--unless you are in a hurry, wait for a commercial barge to go through with. The locks are about 5 miles apart so there aren't that many to do in a day.

Whether in Germany or any other country, working the variety of locks is a time-honored tradition that adds a unique flavor to cruising the waterways of Europe. No doubt da Vinci would be proud to see the magnificent waterway network spawned by his creative energies.

Chapter 6

MEETING AND OVERTAKING OTHER BOATS

Cruising the canals and rivers of Europe is truly tranquil and simple. It would be even more simple if you never had to meet another boat, especially not another barge, and more especially not a mammoth barge. Those few ripples of tension on your otherwise blissfully calm river of tranquillity will definitely come--I guarantee you--as you encounter another craft. The following techniques are intended to make your "other boat" encounters as cordial as possible--as you meet them, overtake them, and are overtaken by them.

MEETING

Given a choice between a meeting situation or an overtaking situation, meeting is much simpler. It is also by far the most frequent. The amount of challenge involved as you meet another barge depends on the   size of the craft and the size of the canal. The larger the barge and the smaller the canal, the greater the challenge. I know that sounds obvious, but the critical factor here is more than how to steer straight. It's the unseen underwater forces that make the challenge.

Principle: **The bow pushes a wave of water. The propeller first pulls and then pushes**.

As the other craft approaches, your barge will be first pushed, then pulled, and finally pushed again. Here is why.

The bow of the oncoming barge acts like a giant watery bulldozer as it shoves a mass of water in front of it. The water is pushed forward and to the side. It's the side part that will push you--about the time your bows come abreast--toward the bank. This push, however, is deceptive. You will feel your barge being pushed shoreward and will instinctively turn a bit to port, toward the other boat. Catch yourself here. Don't give in to the instinct. Hold the wheel steady despite the push to the side, because what is about to happen is far more significant. Just after the push comes the pull. Instead of being shoved, your barge now is being sucked--right toward the side of the barge now beside you. This suction is a far greater force than the bow wave that pushed you. If you have instinctively given in to the temptation to turn into the barge with the bow wave, you are now in double jeopardy because both your rudder and the suction caused by the two propellers now combine to bring the two barges together.

It is easy to understand how the bow wave pushes. But it is fascinating to discover the dynamics at work in the "pull" that immediately follows the bow wave push. To understand that phenomenon requires a bit of explanation of how a propeller works.

Most of us would think that the propeller pushes the barge through the water. Well, yes, it does...but as the blades turn, the propeller actually **pulls** water from the sides and forward of the boat to feed those hungry blades. As discussed in an earlier chapter, the blades literally suck water from under the boat and push it out the back. Water from the front and sides of the boat flow under it to replace the sucked away water. So every bit of water shoved out the stern has to be sucked from under the boat, and from the front and sides.

A loaded *peniche*, her hull near the canal bottom, meets our barge. Our crew is ready to fend off with a tire if necessary.

Now, when two boats meet, there are two suction fields that confront one another. Both barges pull in water from their sides. What is more, the closer they get to one another, the stronger the suction! It is almost like two vacuum cleaners trying to vacuum each other. So you see why I caution you not to turn into the oncoming barge when being temporarily pushed away by the bow wave.

The best way to reduce the intensity of the suction field is to diminish the cause of the suction--the rotation of the prop. So, well before the approach, slow down...and proceed idle speed in gear.

Good. You have made it through the push of the bow wave and the pull of the prop. Your bow is about to clear the stern of the other barge. Now the third force hits.

As soon as your bow is past the stern of the other barge you get pushed, again. This time the same propeller which sucked at your barge to feed water to its blades now pushes you away with the water it force-fully spews out behind. This churning wash spreads out from the stern in a V pattern. Once again it pushes you to the side, just as the bow wave did.

A good bit of engine thrust--if you are still well clear of the bank--will give you momentum to power through the sideways angular force of the prop wash.

You have now just been pushed-pulled-pushed through the first of in-numerable encounters on your trip. Some will be uneventful, others quite interesting, depending on canal and barge size.

The narrower and the shallower the canal, the less water is readily available to feed the blades of the propeller and the more pronounced will be the suction effect I just described. Many small canals are just a foot or two deeper than the loaded barges that cruise them. In fact, I am told that some stretches of canal, particularly in northern France, are so shal-low that loaded peniches shove their way through the mud, ever so slowly. In conditions like that, the barge displaces so much of the avail-able water as it passes that there is very little water under and around it to feed the propeller. When two barges meet, even more water is dis-placed and even less water is left to feed both propellers. Hence the need to proceed slowly, with engine at idle to curb the propeller's appetite.

On large canals or broad, deep rivers, on the other hand, the effect on your barge as you meet a large vessel is minimal. There is plenty of wa-ter available under both barges and little must come from the sides, which reduces the suction. You will scarcely note the effects I described above and can meet the barge without giving it a thought. (For more on this phenomenon, see Chapter 7, *Rivers and Canals*).

Yet the small picturesque waterways that wind their way through the Dutch countryside, offshoots of the broad main channels, are well worth the extra vigilance required. Besides, the challenge makes them more fun. When you cruise in Belgium or France, nearly all the waterways are shallow and require this kind of care as you meet barges, except for the larger canalized rivers like the Seine, the Rhone, or the Meuse.

To recap, follow these procedures when another vessel approaches in a fairly narrow canal.

1. Hold course near mid-channel at first. Don't get handicapped into the side of the canal and out of control by going over too early.

2. Slow down. Throttle back plenty early. Drop to idle forward.

3. Move to starboard when about five barge lengths separate yours from the oncoming barge. He will do likewise.

4. Don't get too close to the side of the canal or your prop suction will pull your stern into the bank. Plan a course that gives adequate clearance between the two craft but leaves you decently away from the bank.

5. As your bow waves meet (the effect of the wave is real but your speed should be so slow that you cannot see a "wave") both bows will move a little away from each other, which brings both sterns slightly more toward one another. Don't turn toward the other vessel in reaction to the bow wave. Now is the time to hold steady.

6. Accelerate slightly just after the hulls are side by side. It helps your barge develop forward momentum and push away from the other barge.

7. Put your wheel hard to starboard. Why? The prop wash (the final push) will try to shove your stern into the bank and your biceps will get exercised as you work the wheel to keep the barge straight in the canal.

8. Now be very careful. You are in the V-shaped propeller wash of the barge you just met. If you now have enough momentum, you can accelerate right through his wash without being pushed into the

We met this unloaded barge while her skipper stopped for lunch

dangerous shallow water near the bank. Make a judgment call here. You need to either power up to churn through the wake, or, if there is any doubt the prop may hit the bank, place the gearshift in neutral and let the prop wash shove you into the bank. It will take a few moments of patience while you pole off and continue on your way, but that sure beats a broken or bent propeller blade! Prudence and caution are the key words here. Your judgment will sharpen with each passing barge, and there will be many.

One final word before we leave the barge encounter subject. Be alert for the "blue flag" rule. When an upstream barge (or any commercial barge on a canal) displays a one meter by one meter (a little more than a yard) blue square bordered in white on the starboard side of his pilothouse, you must pass him (actually meet him) on the opposite side than you would otherwise expect. Normally, without the blue flag, you would pass just as you would with a car, each keeping to the right. When a blue flag is displayed, however, each keeps to the left. (See also Rules of the Road in Chapter 9, *Cruising Considerations*).

OVERTAKING

When in doubt, don't pass. After all, who is in a hurry? If you have the urge to rush, rush, rush, your frame of mind is not on canal cruising, it's still on that LA freeway.

On most waterways, especially the smaller ones, all boats and barges go one speed anyway. It is the speed limit set to reduce the stern wake and the wash that erodes the canal banks and shallows the canal. For example, the speed limit on the Burgundy Canal in France is six kilometers per hour (about three and one-half miles per hour); on the Nivernais Canal in the same region, the limit is eight kilometers per hour. Everyone pretty much abides by the speed limit except for an occasional irresponsible hot shot. If you were one of those, you wouldn't take the time to study this book.

But there will be rare circumstances when overtaking is both prudent and necessary.

Adequate clearance is critical as you pass, because the same forces at work when barges meet are at work when you pass, or are being passed. The difference is the time interval. When barges meet, each is going the opposite direction and the time that the suction forces have to work on each other is brief. They are in and out of the field in a few seconds. However, when one barge overtakes another, both are going the same direction and therefore the length of exposure to all three forces--push, pull, push--is more pronounced. That is why overtaking should only be done with plenty of clearance and preferably on deep, wide waterways.

If you must pass another barge or boat, overtake very slowly. Put fenders out to starboard as a precaution. Stay as close to the opposite bank as possible to maximize the distance between the two craft. As you pull abreast, nurse the engine in and out of neutral to minimize the suction effect of your propeller. Once you are past the other boat, ease the throttle forward very slowly to minimize the effect of your prop wash on the other craft.

BEING OVERTAKEN

You will be overtaken by commercial barges on the larger waterways. The speed limits on these big arterials, unlike the smaller canals, are higher and the superpowered barges simply go faster. Unlike you and I, they have deadlines to meet and time is money. They are bigger, faster, and you should stay out of their way. It is professional courtesy.

When you travel the larger commercial arterial waterways, practice neck exercises. Either install a rear view mirror in the pilothouse or else rotate your head with regularity to "check six". These behemoths are huge, have tremendous momentum and, if inattention on the helm causes you to inadvertently wander into their path as they overtake, they have neither the brakes nor the maneuverability to prevent an accident. Be alert!

In addition, if these barges are larger than yours, they probably have a larger engine to drive a larger propeller, which means more water is sucked in to feed the propeller. Do not be misled by my statement a few paragraphs earlier that meeting a large commercial barge on a broad waterway will have little noticeable effect. Because of the length of time you are exposed to the suction forces, the effect on your barge while she is being passed can be considerable.

The Rhine is a mighty river with plenty of water. Father Rhine also has plenty of magnificent barges equipped with sufficient power to counter the swift river currents as they churn upstream through the Lorelei, the impressive gorge from Koblenz to Bingen. These great waterborne beasts push, pull and push immense amounts of water.

We were overtaken by a large commercial barge as we cruised downstream on the Rhine. We had just passed under the same section of a bridge, which brought our two barges closer than I otherwise would have preferred. Still, we were separated by a good 100 feet and I felt reasonably comfortable. As the big barge's bow pulled even with our stern I felt his bow wave push us a bit more away from him, which increased the comfort factor. Now he pulled even with me. I noticed the 100 feet was now 80, 70, 60, 50...and suddenly I was less than one boat length (my boat length!) away from him. Our rate of closure was faster than his rate of overtaking. Our craft was drawn into the suction field created by his immense water-consuming propeller.

I looked up at the skipper and he looked down on me. With care, I nosed my barge away from him and toward the shore, aware that this action turned my rudder and swung my stern toward him...now about 30 feet away. Though I was at our cruising speed on the Rhine (about 12 km/hr), our 165 horsepower engine had a good reserve of power. I used it. I pushed the handle far forward and felt the motor respond with a surge of power, as it strove to overcome the propeller-induced current drawing us into his hulk.

I can't tell for sure, but it seemed the skipper of the big barge, aware of the situation, backed off on his power somewhat so as to reduce the strength of the suction and help facilitate our escape. Once we accelerated at an angle away from him, we cleared without incident. We exchanged respectful waves.

Because we were on the wide Rhine, the final push of his propeller (the push to the side by his V wash once he had passed us) did not affect us adversely. It moved us more to the side, but we were far from the shore.

On waterways smaller than the Rhine, barges normally pass more slowly--the smaller the canal, the slower and more careful the rate of overtake. But the dynamics are the same.

When being overtaken on a fairly small waterway by a barge, I recommend these procedures:

1. **Move toward the right** half of the canal with a **definite movement**. That alerts the barge skipper that you are aware of his overtaking presence.

2. **Slow somewhat**. Usually not as slow as for meeting, but enough to get him by as quickly as possible and reduce the amount of time your barge is subject to the pull of his prop. In very small canals, come to a virtual standstill and the barge will overtake you very slowly.

3. **Keep your transmission in forward** to maintain way and control. The faster the overtaking barge, the faster you must be to avoid being pulled into his hull. You need to strike a balance here. Travel slowly enough to get him by quickly; yet retain sufficient speed to resist his pull. As a general rule, it is better to be a bit slower at first so you can accelerate out of his pull as he passes.

4. Just before his stern passes your bow, **your bow may be drawn** toward his stern by his suction. As long as your bow misses his stern, there is no problem, because this points your barge back toward the center of the waterway and puts you in a good position to avoid the shoreward thrust of his prop wash.

5. Depending on how close your stern is to the shore after the overtaking barge clears your hull, either **accelerate** back into the center of the

canal, or allow yourself to **drift** into the bank in neutral, pole off, and resume your cruise.

Incidentally, have your crew put out heavy duty fenders on the port side when you see you are about to be overtaken, as a precaution in case you are drawn into his hull. Then tell them to stay away from that side. Sometimes a conscientious crewmember will do strange things in an emergency. Tell them beforehand that if you are headed for a nudge, they should never, never, never, get their hands or feet anywhere near the point of impact. I have noted it before and I emphasize it again. Steel is strong. It is a lot stronger and much more fixable than human limbs. Besides, hand and arms won't do much against umpteen tons of bulk.

Most often when you are overtaken you will not be cruising down the canal. You will be moored by the side of the canal, as is the common practice throughout Europe (see Chapter 4, *Mooring*). A barge will pass. Watch your barge carefully as the barge passes. You will see a live demonstration of each of the forces discussed here.

First, the push of the bow wave will cause your barge to strain at her mooring lines as she moves in the same direction as the overtaking barge. Next, the bow wave will be immediately followed by the pull of the screw suction we discussed. Now your barge will strain the opposite direction with greater force, as she simultaneously attempts to pull away from the bank as if the overtaking barge is a long lost lover. Finally, the wash from the thrusting prop will push your barge back against the bank, and she once again will strain against her lines.

Chapter 4 discussed techniques of mooring that handle surges from passing craft. I mention it again to underscore the impact your barge has on moored craft. To keep friends and influence people positively, please drive slowly (if possible in neutral) when cruising past moored boats. The smaller the moored boat, of course, the greater your effect. Elementary canal cruising courtesy says go slow when passing moored boats.

Don't worry if right now you don't remember the list of recommended actions to be taken as you meet, pass, and are overtaken. But this is important: To know, understand, and visualize the push of the bow wave, the pull of the propeller, and the V-shaped push of its wash. Being able to picture these will enable you to respond to any "other barge encounter". The procedures are based on those principles and are designed to make the learning curve trouble free.

Chapter 7

RIVERS AND CANALS

There is walking versus running, downhill versus cross-country skiing, and sailing versus water skiing. And then there is river cruising versus canal cruising.

Rivers are broad and deep, canals are usually narrow and shallow. There's is no speed limit for barging on rivers. Canals impose their own limits. Rivers either boost progress or slow it with their current. Canals--and this may surprise you--always have an adverse current, as I will explain later. Rivers have carved their own channels through the millennia, while canals are man-made and merely centuries old. Moorages are selected quite carefully on rivers, since you don't simply pick any old spot to tie up as on canals.

But more than anything else, there is a different mood, a totally different feeling that comes from river cruising versus canal cruising, symbolized somewhat by the fact that the broad rivers allow one to lay back in the captain's chair and steer with your toes while canal cruising particularly in the smaller canals, requires that you lean slightly forward in your chair, intent on keeping the barge headed straight.

Cruisable rivers are most common in Germany (the Rhine, Mosel, Neckar, Main, Lahn), then France (Rhone, Moselle, Meuse, Seine, and Oise are the major ones), then the Netherlands (Maas, Waal, Ijssel, Vecht), and finally Belgium (Meuse, Scheldt, and the incomparable Leie).

Route planning should definitely take rivers into consideration. Whenever possible, cruise downstream. The current makes a huge difference in speed over ground and fuel consumption, especially on the unharnessed Rhine north of the Black Forest and the same river as it enters Holland, where it is called the Waal. No dams or locks impede the flow of this mighty river. Upstream passages should be avoided at its two fastest sections: the famous Lorelei or Rhine gorge from Bingen to Koblenz, and from the Black Forest to Karlsruhe. Sustained rainfall combined with spring snowmelt also drastically influence the speed of the river current. This is particularly true of France's Rhone river, where currents of 10 knots are sometimes recorded.

Relaxed "steering by the toe" cruising on the France's River Doubs

Running downstream, however, makes these rivers a joy ride. Through careful planning we ran downstream on nearly all rivers. The one upstream section of about 15 miles on the free flowing Waal from Nijmegen to its junction with the Ijssel reminded us why it is smart to avoid many of these labored sections. On the other hand, powering upstream on the frequently locked/dammed Neckar and Mosel/Moselle was far different, only slightly affecting our progress.

Europe's large rivers historically have carried commercial traffic year round and they remain vital commercial arterials today. This is where the big boys run, stacked sometimes three stories tall with containers, their pilothouses perched on gigantic scissors-shaped hydraulic shafts which elevate them above their loads. Multiple barges joined into one are also common on the rivers, where we have seen as many as four peniches fused together for labor-saving economy. The best advice about the great commercial barges I received was from a German *"Wasserschutzpolizei"* (water police): *"Stay out of their way"*.

That is fine in theory, just as the best advice on how to avoid trucks on the Interstate is to stay out of their way. To do so, however, it is important to know where you are supposed to be, so there are no surprises. There is a designated position for you on the river, which is alluded to in Chapter 6 and discussed in more detail in Chapter 9, under "Rules of the Road". Yet it is sufficiently important to re-emphasize here.

The rules are simple but critical, and there are only three. First, keep all red buoys to starboard (keep them on your right, or stay to the left of them) when going downstream. Second, stay to the right side of the channel. Third, observe the "blue flag" rule.

The "blue flag" is a one meter square blue panel with a white border and a flashing white light in the center that signals "lane switch". Instead of staying to the right side of the channel, vessels must switch to the left side. The decision to fly the "blue flag" is made by the boat heading upstream because he is negotiating the curves and fighting the current. The downstream boat (the one headed downstream) must respect whatever the upstream boat (headed upstream) determines.

The challenge riding downstream on Europe's great rivers is to detect the "blue flaggers" at the earliest opportunity. One may be relaxed and steering with toes, but binoculars must always be at the ready. As soon as a barge rounds a bend ahead, focus on the starboard side of her pilothouse to check for the "blue flag".

Things get spicy when you encounter a group of barges, some overtaking, some "blue flagging" and some not. On the Rhine, we had to thread the needle several times. Our 70 foot barge seemed like a toy between the massive churning monstrosities powering upstream on either side. Believe me, when the current is hurtling you down on these huge vessels, there is no time to start reading up on the "Rules of the Road". You need to know where to go and then stay there.

I want to highlight another important aspect of river cruising. It applies to piloting in canals as well as rivers, but river current speed underlines its importance: telegraph your path early on. Barges don't turn on a dime, so it is very important to signal intentions to an oncoming barge. If you are in the middle of the river when that big barge comes round the bend flying the "blue flag", immediately move decidedly and obviously to port, thereby letting the barge know without a doubt that you know which side of the channel to be on and there is no question about your moving there.

The same holds true if you make a mistake and are caught on the wrong side. Let's say you are coming downstream, rounding a tight bend to the left, and "cutting the corner". You are on the left hand side of the channel with restricted visibility because of the river bend. Suddenly you see a massive bow come into view around the bend, not far ahead. Is he "blue flagging"? You won't know until the pilothouse comes into view. Now, you really should have been on the right hand side of the channel where the rules say you should be and where you would have good visibility of oncoming traffic in a left hand turn. But you are not.

Do you cut across his bow to get to the right hand side? And then what if halfway across you discover he is "blue flagging"? Do you then double-back to the left hand side?

Or do you hug the port shore, hoping for the best?

There is a reason I can visualize this situation so well. I decided the safest course was to stay out of the way of the big barge and to let him know in no uncertain terms that, even though I belonged on the opposite side of the channel, I was definitely going to stay where I was. As his pilothouse came into view (no "blue flag"), I gave a pronounced turn hugging the left hand bank even tighter.

We passed without incident, though the crew tossed me a glance that needed no translation and the lock master came out at the next lock to ask to see my papers. No doubt the skipper had reported that a crazy American was loose on the waterways and didn't know the rules of the road.

Chastened, I was more careful on my position around river bends after that.

Mooring on rivers is more limited than on canals. As discussed in more detail in Chapter 4, *Mooring*, always moor facing upstream, and always note your position relative to the nearest lock. Especially when cruising in the spring, remember that sudden rainfalls and warm weather can bring the river rising quickly, and that the closer you are to a lock downstream of you, the better. Conversely, if a lock is just upstream, you are more vulnerable to a rising river level. Therefore, mooring lines should be as long as possible to accommodate changes in the river level. Whenever you leave the barge keep the weather in the back of your mind, especially if you leave the barge for the weekend.

Be aware of any passing commercial barges as you near the mooring site. Their push-pull-push effect can be dangerous if it hits just as your crew is lassoing a ring or bollard. And, of course, after you tie down, observe the effect from one or two passing barges to see how well your mooring job stands up. It seems that the biggest rivers and the biggest barges, which give your mooring technique the toughest challenges, are in Germany.

Cruising in Germany means river cruising, with the exception of the northern plains, where the flatter topography facilitates canals. These are mainly constructed in an east-west direction to tie together the northerly flowing rivers. With the great Father Rhine, the beautiful Neckar, the vineyard-sloped gorge of the Mosel, the winding Main, and the idyllic Lahn, southern and central Germany is a land of flowing waters and spectacular scenery.

The Rhine, of course, is the mightiest of them all. Unless your barge has plenty of power and you want to try the upstream stretch from Holland to the Mosel at Koblenz, the normal point of entry into the Rhine will be at Strasbourg, where one enters the canalized section between Basel, Switzerland and the northern edge of the Black Forest.

Give some thought before you enter the German rivers, however. With the exception of the Mosel and the canals of northern Germany, the only way to get to the German rivers is to first cruise the Rhine; and the Rhine is the serious domain of mighty waters, huge barges, and a protective *Polizei* (police). The river and the barges are manageable, as long as you know what you are doing. But the German *Polizei*, or more officially "*Wassershutzpolizei*", are a different matter. They may exclude you from cruising or they may help you. If they want to exclude you, I suspect they have enough rules on the books to do so.

I have read about many of these regulations but the key one you may need to cite, should the occasion warrant, is the one which says the German government will respect the licensing and regulations of the country of the skipper's origin--a very key rule.

I remember well the incredulous look on the face of the young waterway police officer when I told him we had no mandatory licenses in the USA. *How can we be civilized and have no such rules?* his look seemed to say. *How can we put a man on the moon and have no mandatory skipper licenses?* Knowing the German penchant for paperwork, I had wisely stuffed my attache case with as many bits of boating related paper as I could assemble: my Waikiki channel check card, Washington State boat dealer card, and sailing school certificates (I own a sailing school firm). I supplemented these with a quick litany of my offshore and European cruising experience. When he asked if I knew how the locks worked it seemed to help when I mentioned matter-of-factly that I had transited over 300 of them by that time. Having cruised successfully through Holland, Belgium, and France without incident, he concluded we would not likely be a hazard on the German rivers and let us proceed. I know he passed the word upriver to his colleagues because we found the courteous blue water police boats keeping a cordial eye on us from then on.

Because so few recreational boats venture into the German rivers-- again with the exception of the Mosel--it is difficult to get charts of the rivers. A kindly German boater spending the weekend in Strasbourg lent me his Rhine charts. Once we had cruised as far as Heidelberg, I found cruising guides, all in German of course, to each of her rivers. Despite the language difference, the river guides are adequate because of their good drawings of the rivers and city facilities. If you don't have German charts, drive to a chandlery in Germany or Holland or, well before you leave, contact the nearest German consulate in the US.

As you enter the Rhine canal in Strasbourg, France, northbound, there will be almost no downstream current through the locked sections. After you go through several huge locks in this international waterway on the German/French border, you enter the real River Rhine near the northern end of the Black Forest. The current effect is immediate.

Engineers have installed underwater berms or levees along many sections of the river to prevent bank erosion. Made of heavy rock, many jut out into the stream for 25 to 50 meters from either side. Red and green buoys mark the east and west side of the river channel, respectively, but they are often set as much as ten or twenty feet inside the berms. In other words, give the buoys plenty of berth. Those underwater berms would clip off a propeller or damage even a strong steel hull.

As the Rhine continues north, it leaves the French-German border and enters Germany proper. At the Baden Baden station, located in a tiny harbor on the east bank, German border officials either wave you through or signal you to turn into the little harbor for a customs check. If they signal you in, be sure to do a 180 and enter the harbor while coming upstream. Otherwise the momentum of the current--very swift at that point--will run your barge up on the bank at the entrance to the harbor, an inauspicious entry into the country. The opening borders of the European Community may eliminate this challenging inspection station in the future.

The current is very swift between the border station and Karlsruhe, where one can find anchorage in small harbors on both sides of the river.

The Rhine is the most difficult of all the rivers for mooring due to its strong current and lack of facilities for smaller barges. The harbors along the Rhine are chiefly for the big boys, though smaller barges can often manage to share them. City walls are also far more difficult to use on the Rhine than those of cities on the other rivers. Due to current and flooding, walls are usually constructed farther back on the bank, where waters are too shallow in normal conditions.

Most marinas are located in protected harbors just off the Rhine and are designed for small boats. They charge several marks per meter per night.

Just past Mannheim lies the confluence of the Rhine and the Neckar. The picturesque Neckar begins to show her beauty at Heidelberg. She is navigable to Stuttgart, a modern industrial city which rose literally from the rubble of allied bombing in World War II. There is little of historical interest or beauty along the big commercial jetties in Stuttgart, but the jewels along the way at Besigheim, Neckargemund, Heilbronn, Eberbach, and many other riverside villages make it indeed worthwhile to cruise this storied land of castles and quaintness.

Further north along the Rhine, the Lahn tempts. We lacked the time to take this river, used primarily by recreational craft, but it comes very highly recommended.

By turning right on the Main River, near Frankfurt, one may now begin a great odyssey. The upper reaches of the Main in the area of Nuremberg, heading toward Austria, now serve as the link between the two great watersheds of Europe--the Rhine watershed draining northern Europe through Holland and into the North Sea, and the Danube watershed, which begins at a spring high in the Black Forest and drains southeastern Europe into the Black Sea.

The first dirt for what is now the Main-Donau (Danube) Canal was dug in 793 by the crews of the emperor Charlemagne. Its opening these many centuries later had been scheduled and rumored and postponed for a number of years. "Any year now" was the latest word we received while cruising there. German waterway officials told us in 1991 that the acquisition of former East Germany was draining off so much capital that the Main-Donau Canal was being postponed yet once again. Finally, the completion of this grand uniting of the two great east and west watersheds occurred in September 1992.

If cruising through the Czech Republic, Slovakia, Austria, Hungary, Romania, and Bulgaria appeals to you, you were born in the right century. Check thoroughly into mooring facilities and fees in the former communist countries before you depart, however.

A more conventional and certainly very popular river for cruising is the spectacular Mosel, the German portion of which is the more beautiful and runs from the historic Roman city of Trier to Koblenz. The river winds serpentine-like through a jagged gorge with steep vineyarded sides--so steep the tractors perched high above the river cannot be used for cultivation. Their power take-offs turn a reel around which is wound a cable, used to raise and lower the farmers up and down the sides of the gorge as they cultivate, prune, fertilize, and harvest the grapes which make the world's most famous white wines--like the *Piesporter Gold-tropchen Trockenbeerenauslese*!

Cities along the Mosel have discovered moorage fees are a revenue source and you may well have to pay among the higher rates in Europe for a berth along the quay. Even so, they are decidedly less expensive than most American marinas.

CANALS

It is simple but nevertheless true. Canals come in two sizes, large and small, with very few in-betweens.

Large Canals

Large canals are in the lowlands, primarily in the Netherlands (which means "lowlands"). Two large canal fingers also poke south to Antwerp and to Brussels, in Belgium, and large east-west canals in northern Germany link the north flowing rivers. Construction is set to begin soon to enlarge the Canal du Rhon au Rhin canal along the scenic valley of the River Doubs in eastern France. This link will allow large efficient commercial barges to run from the North Sea to the Mediterranean, using the Rhine and Rhone Rivers. And finally, the great Main-Donau canal permits large transport from Rotterdam to the Black Sea.

Cruising the large canals resembles cruising large rivers, except for the lack of current or dams. They are broad and deep. One can relax and steer by the toes--but one must also be "on their toes" to avoid the swift large vessels.

Small Canals

One can seldom lean back in the chair on the "*peniche*" sized canals of France, Belgium, and Holland. These narrow canals with their penchant for beckoning your stern toward one side or the other call for alert, careful steering.

It is easy to get into trouble on canal curves in particular. The sliding effect described in Chapter 2, *Torque*, can bring your barge, and especially the vulnerable propeller perilously close to the far bank.

I feel more comfortable anticipating the turn with the bow. It works for me. But a friend of mine uses what I call the "Vander Griend technique", doubtless derived from some ancestral barging bloodline. He figures if the stern stays out of trouble, the barge stays out of trouble. So he steers looking over his shoulder to keep the *stern in the middle of the channel*. And this works for him.

It also works, he says, to determine where the deepest channel within the canal lies. Sometimes one bank of the canal has eroded more than the other, which makes one side of the canal shallower than the other. He watches for the self-induced current, described below, and places his stern so that the speed of induced current is equal on both sides of the barge. The propeller, he deduces correctly, is thus placed squarely in the center of the deepest channel of the canal.

So "steer by bow" or "steer by stern", whatever you find works best for you. The end result is the same--to keep the barge in the middle of the channel and keep the propeller far from bankside rocks.

Self-Induced Current

If you were to leave a river for a canal, particularly a smaller canal, you might expect the current to stop as well. But it doesn't. Although you can carefully plan your itinerary so you always go downstream on the rivers, it may seem like you are always going upstream in the canals.

On one of our first days cruising on the barge Justin kept noting, "*Look, Dad, we're going upstream.*" He was right. If fact, we always seemed to be going upstream. I looked at the grass and leaves floating at the canal sides. They were always moving the opposite direction we were. Then I peered carefully farther forward. All was still. Strange, I thought. Are the waters against us? All so calm and then suddenly rushing to push against us as soon as we approach? Is this a subtle sabotage designed by European waterways against a vessel flying the

American flag? A bit of objective analysis, however, convinced us that the principles of physics were transcontinental. Yes, we were cruising upstream, because our prop, by *pulling* the water from under the boat, was creating the upstream current!

We found that the faster we turned the prop (the higher the engine RPMs), the more contrary current we generated. So the faster we tried to go, the slower we went (kind of). (Some would find a universal life principle at work here.) We found that each canal had a speed appropriate to its size. Whenever the prop-generated contrary current became too fast, we slowed down. It seems that canals operate as their own traffic cop. Try to go too fast for the conditions, and they throw current to climb through. Persist in your transgression and, like a cop, they will literally pull you over. You will suddenly find torque overcoming forward thrust as you start to slide sideways down the canal, as if the canal is saying "*Hey, pull over!*"; as it should. Excess speed on the canal not only reduces efficiency by generating an upstream current but also produces a nasty stern wave that can seriously erode the bank.

Continuous erosion is one of the most pervasive and expensive canal problems faced by European governments as they work to keep the canals operative. Every bit of bank eroded into the canal becomes a bit on the bottom that must be laboriously and expensively retrieved by a dredger. You can let the smaller canals dictate the speed limit for you by watching for a self-generated adverse current and the bank eroding stern wave.

Dutch Canals

Of all the nations of western Europe, I doubt if any country provides as much diversity of cruising canals as does Holland. She has large commercial arterials like the Princess Margreet Canal and the Zwartewater where barges can run at maximum speed with no noticeable self-induced current and no stern wave. But they also have tiny rural canals that wend their way through green pastures of grazing sheep and Holstein dairy cattle. And they have everything in between.

The verdant, picturesque canals of western Overijssel province and Friesland, in northern Holland, are a favorite of cruising Europeans. The

Kalenberger Kracht in particular is a gorgeous if challenging wriggle past flowering gardens and perfectly kept thatch-roofed brick country homes. Many of the villages are community hubs to the surrounding farmland and others are historic cities that you can cruise right into and park your home on main street. The canals in southern Holland, below Amsterdam, cut through more heavily populated areas. On them you can visit the famous Keukenhof Tulip Gardens and cruise by rows of windmills whose great arms still scrape the sky.

Recall that these windmills historically have removed excess water from the land, pumped it into ditches, and then from ditches into canals so they can flow to the sea. As a consequence, the canals of Holland are frequently lifted above the surrounding countryside, giving a panoramic view as you glide above it all. Your view is unimpeded even by electric and telephone poles since all such lines have been buried by the orderly Dutch, except for the major transmission lines on steel towers. The effect is startling, lending a clean garden manicured look to the green Dutch surroundings..

You can moor almost anywhere on Holland's canals, especially on her smaller ones. They are quiet, peaceful, and enjoyable--if you don't mind waking up to a cow peering in the window. If you prefer, tie up to the city walls on one of the many canals or rivers that enter virtually every city you may wish to visit.

Belgian Canals

Things aren't quite as neat and tidy in the more industrialized Belgium as in Holland, reflecting perhaps the fact that some of the country seems to be built, like the city of Charleroi, on mountains of coal. Belgium has recently embarked on an overdue, but apparently serious schedule of environmental reconstruction. Although a few of her canals are virtually impassable from stink and sludge, most are acceptable. They lack, however, the maintenance, attractiveness, and order of the Dutch canals. Still, their canal system connects to one of our all time favorite cities, Brugge, where you can moor in a canal spur in the city and luxuriate in the pervasive splendor and charm of this formerly wealthy Hanseatic League city--no, not city really. Although the old city is large enough to be called that, it has a unique cultured village charm unrivaled in all of Europe.

South of Brussels, just after the hills begin their rise from the lowlands, lies one of the intriguing phenomena--reportedly one of only two in the world--of the European canal network. The Roncieres inclined plane is covered in more detail in Chapter 5, *Locks*. Take it if you have a chance. It's unforgettable.

One is less inclined to stop and push in the pins along a picturesque bank for an overnight mooring in Belgium. Many of the larger canals in Flanders have sloping concrete sides and the smaller ones just don't seem that inviting. Most often, one moors on the lock approaches or in the cities, except Brussels, whose more beautiful points of entry are definitely *not* from canalside. We did not encounter any mooring fees in Belgium, outside marinas, except for certain areas in the beautiful city of Namur.

Although the northern province of Flanders began charging for using its canals in 1991, there is no charge in the hillier, southern and Francophile province of Belgium, Wallonia (as of this writing). Nor is there any charge on the international waterway, the Meuse River, the most popular way through Belgium. It cuts through both Flanders and Wallonia, but in so doing bypasses both the beautiful and the ugly in this land of friendly and most helpful people. With the renowned hospitality of her people, some of the finest food on the continent, and wonderful medieval cities, Belgium has the potential to become a barge cruising jewel--when she cuts the grass, cleans up the trash, and restores her creation.

French Canals

This is still the fabled land of exotic canals and cities of romance. It is also a nation of locks as the east-west canals rise up to the plateaus that form the broad backbone of France. That these canals exist at all is testimony to the vision of her leaders. For these are not lowlands that need to be drained. These are mountains that are being crossed; well, rolling hills, at least.

Included in Napoleon's vision of a commercially united Europe (only now being realized) was a standardized lock system. Except on rivers, where larger locks now accommodate the barges of today, the French canal system is characterized by the size that will accommodate the 38.5 meter long, 5 meter wide "*peniches*".

Because of the number of locks on the canals--sometimes every 1/2 mile for extended stretches--cruising in France takes time.

France has many canal networks to choose from, and each has its own character that needs to be sampled and savored. Among the most popular are the Burgundy/Nivernais canals in central eastern France, and the Canal du Midi in southern France. The Midi lies in the drier and mostly warmer region that reflects more of a Mediterranean flavor in both topography and architecture than the canal systems in the central area of the country. The story of the Midi's construction is an intriguing tale of royal politics and the vision of Pierre Paul Riquet, a salt tax collector whose engineering genius exceeded the best minds of previous centuries, including even the renowned Leonardo da Vinci. This tax man's remarkable feat created a slice of water uniting the Atlantic (Bay of Biscay) with the Mediterranean.

It really is very hard to rate the different canal systems of France. Before we entered France, we asked fellow Americans who had cruised the European canals from spring to fall each year for the past eight to rate 'the best'. Hoping for a clear recommendation, we were somewhat frustrated when they could not give a ranking. *It depends upon what types of things you like*, they said. *You almost have to taste to find out what you like.* Only after coursing through many of them would we conclude they were right.

Nevertheless, there are some highlights that stand out for us. The run from Nancy (spectacular *Place de Stanislas*) to Strasbourg (fascinating city but hazardous mooring) has some memorable sections, including Europe's other inclined plane lock, some gorgeous cities and a sampling of both French and German culture.

The stretch from the wonderful walled medieval city of Toul eastward crosses a broad scenic valley.

The canalized Oise (pronounced "waaz") north and west of Paris traverses through the land of artists (Van Gogh, Monet), though one must venture off the canal to really breathe the beauty of this region.

Those with at least a month for cruising can make a round trip using the Burgundy ("*Bourgogne*" in French) and quaint Nivernais canals as the stem of a loop either to the west or to the east, depending upon preference and time.

Then there are the Ardennes, the canalized Meuse through Verdun, the Canal du Centre, and many others.

Moorings in France, like Holland, are pretty much wherever one would like to stop, although most prefer to moor in a village to sample its delights, or at the approaches to a lock. The government has sponsored construction of small city harbors, usually a city wall with bollards and sometimes with grass and picnic benches for recreational bargers. For many years there was no charge to use these. Recently, however, some villages have cast an envious eye on a revenue source and charge a modest fee. Yet, one has to sit back in wonder and appreciation that we have access to this intriguing and awe inspiring network of canals, and until 1993 we recreational bargers have had to pay nearly nothing for its use. When you think about the considerable expense involved in the maintenance of this vast enterprise, and the services from hundreds of seen and unseen canal workers, we can only say thanks to these countries for their hospitality. This intricate network of waterways takes care, planning, and plenty of maintenance.

Yes, maintenance. If you thought Belgian canals needed repair, just wait until you get to France. The French have a tough job trying to keep pace with the stern wake erosion of hundreds of little fiberglass charter "bargettes", or "*penichettes*" as they like to call them. You will see a variety of bank retention devices employed in the war against bank erosion: cement bags, filled tires, blocks, wood planks. But the most common are interlocking sheets of steel driven into the canal sides by pile drivers.

For all the canals, there is one contribution we bargers and future bargers can make. Slow down. Avoid erosion from the stern wake.

TUNNELS

One place where barges for sure go slow is in a tunnel. And France has several. We transited seven of them in that country; the longest was three miles long. They are all one way and the longer ones normally allow one direction in the morning, the opposite in the afternoon. Some of the longer ones have escorts or tugs, though both times we paid for a tug, we were told to use our own power. The tunnel on the Burgundy canal is fairly small as far as height and sides is concerned, so be sure to check the graphic available at the first lock on the Burgundy Canal to match against your barge's dimensions.

We prepare to pierce a French summit

The tunnels are normally at the summit of a plateau or "mountain" range. Upon emerging from a tunnel, you can count on the locks following being descending ones.

Some tunnels are lit, others completely dark. Even those with lights seem to have several lights in succession burned out, which is enough to throw off one's orientation for steering. When the barge hits the wood planked rail on the side, as inevitably happens, put the transmission in neutral and let the momentum slow until the hull gradually drifts away from the side. Remember that the suction of the prop hugs the hull to the rail. Frankly, that is why it is so difficult to steer in a tunnel. The sides are so narrow and the amount of water is so limited that steering through a tunnel is more of a balancing act than a driving test. You need to balance the propeller in the center of the channel, being aware of its tendency to move either to port or starboard, depending upon its right hand or left hand turning shaft.

There are three important factors to keep in mind for tunnels. First, go plenty slow, probably one to two miles per hour. Second, keep the prop in the center of the channel. This is best done by keeping the bow in the center of the channel. Avoid hard rudder, at least until you sense the stern is being sucked toward the side, in which case you need strong rudder to try to return it to the center. Once the stern has attached itself to the side, however, return the rudder to nearly straight as, with the transmission in neutral, you gently coax the barge away from the side. Third, look far enough ahead in the tunnel to steer the boat in the center.

I should emphasize this last point. Remember the student driver illustration in which the student tends to look at the pavement immediately in front of the car instead of several hundred feet in front of the car? If the student keeps their vision far enough ahead, the steering is more natural. The same is true for a barge in a tunnel. Focus about 100 to 200 feet ahead. How do you do that in a lightless tunnel?

First you must have night vision. It takes 30 minutes to fully develop night vision. Looking slightly out the side of your eye provides better night vision than looking straight ahead. Avoid any bright lights in the barge or on deck. If the barge is equipped with a spotlight, aim it far up the tunnel and away from your eyes. Lacking a spotlight, rig something to show the centerline of the barge without blinding you with a white light.

Not having a spotlight, we chose a cooking pan from the galley and shined the bottom. Then I borrowed my son Danny's little red kerosene lantern, one of those inexpensive ones seemingly available anywhere in the world. Danny lit it and placed it on the anchor windlass forward. The boys carefully laid the pan on its side, its open top facing back toward me. The bottom of the pan laid just aft of the lantern so it shielded the flame from my eyes while the shiny bottom reflected the lantern light forward, lending a soft illumination to the walls and ceiling of the tunnel. Finally, I laid a bright clear plastic covered bicycle locking cable within my field of view alongside the pan. Its glitter picked up the lantern light so it glowed luminescently, giving me a centerline "sight" to keep aimed down the center of the tunnel. It was light enough to see easily but not enough to affect my night vision.

Finally, all lights below being extinguished, I turned on a light in a forward bedroom so its light shone through the round side ports onto the immediate sides of the tunnel. While slowly cruising through the tunnel, I concentrated primarily straight ahead, keeping the glowing cable directly under the highest point of the tunnel ceiling and therefore directly in the center of the channel. Occasionally I shot a quick glance where the light from the bedroom windows played on the concrete tunnel walls, judging from the diameter of the light circle how close we were to each side. Between these two orientations, I was able to keep the barge in the center of the tunnel--*almost* always.

When nearing the end of the tunnel, the proverbial light at the end of the tunnel is blinding. You may wish to tape a small round piece of paper on the pilothouse window to save your vision for the last half mile or so. Or you can place one hand in front of your eyes whenever you look forward.

Shorter tunnels pose few of these difficulties, though they always are longer than they seem when you first see the end approaching. Entry to these shorter tunnels is usually controlled by traffic lights.

Some of the larger tunnels charge for passing through--about $15 at this writing.

The tunnels add interest and a bit of intrigue to the trip, though we always welcomed the wonderful daylight at the end of the tunnel.

If you get the chance, inquire about the history and construction of tunnels you cruise through. Each represents a tremendous engineering accomplishment and seems to have no shortage of fascinating history as well as a curious bit of folklore associated with it.

The tunnels are but one aspect of the ever changing variety in the tremendous network of canals which lay as a lacework across the continent.

Whether cruising among the giant vessels on the mightiest of the great rivers, or slowly poking your nose between the reed-lined banks of the tiniest pasture-parting canal, you will discover each presents its own joys, its own ambiance, as well as its own unique challenges to your cruising skills.

Chapter 8

EQUIPMENT

PACKING GLAND

The engine generates the power and the shaft delivers it to the propeller. On the way, however, it must pierce the hull of the barge through a fitting that keeps the water out while not damaging the shaft. A variety of fittings are used on sailboats and powerboats. On barges, the grease packing gland is the through-hull fitting of choice. In a grease packing gland, the shaft passes through a pipe-like fitting which has a hose attached to the side of it. The hose leads to a large cylinder with a threaded shaft and a handle, called a grease gun. Turning the handle forces grease out the cylinder, through the hose and into the pipe-like fitting. The engine shaft rotates in a sea of captive grease which protects the shaft and forms a watertight seal. Well, most often watertight. A drip every 30 seconds or so doesn't matter, but anything more than that should be given attention before too long. If water is dripping out, so will grease. In fact, it is normal for grease--just a bit--to squeeze out both ends of the shaft packing gland, into the canal and into the barge. Not in large amounts of course, but you should be able to see the ooze nevertheless.

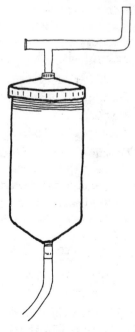

shaft grease gun

Although the number of turns may vary depending upon the equipment, as a general rule take one turn on the grease gun for each hour of engine operation. The bottom line is this: never forget to turn the grease gun for the shaft packing gland. Set up a routine. Many skippers do it immediately after the engine is turned off for the day, because the grease is warm and it is easier to make the turns on the grease gun. When you do it doesn't matter, just make sure you do it.

When you inspect the shaft packing gland, grease should be visible squeezing out of the pipe-like fitting around the shaft. That is a sign it is under pressure, which it must be to work properly.

Periodically, the packing gland needs to be tensioned with the nuts on the leading edge of the gland, but that must be done with care to avoid improper alignment and damage to the shaft. If you are not trained, let a professional do it. Once every year or two is usually often enough, but even then, do it only when excessive grease and more than two water drips a minute come into the barge while the shaft is rotating.

EQUIPMENT MAINTENANCE

Essential maintenance rules are these: Look for grease fittings to lubricate regularly. Change oil and filters on schedule. Keep equipment clean. Read the owner's manuals.

The amount of equipment on a barge seldom approximates that on a cruising sailboat. In addition, floating down a canal or river jars the gear less, to say nothing of the difference in the effect of salt versus fresh water environments on the life of equipment, particularly electronics. Should something break down, help often is not far away.

Nonetheless, prudence dictates adequate spares, particularly of essential items. Many commercial barges carry a spare propeller, since their livelihood depends on staying operational, though few recreational barges carry them.

These are equipment spares I consider wise to carry:
- mooring line
- float switch
- fender (s)
- utility line
- bilge pump
- water pressure pump and pressure switch
- toilet rebuild kit

Keep an eagle eye for any leaks when it rains and grab the heavy duty sealant as soon as the skies clear.

HULL MAINTENANCE

Whether the environment is salt or fresh, boat life aboard a steel vessel is a constant battle against rust. The Dutch sell a wonderful product that chemically changes rust into a bonding substance that acts like a primer. That, plus a chiseling screwdriver, wire brush, sandpaper, touch up paint, small brush and ever vigilant eye form the defensive brigade against this insidious aggressor.

Like most things, rust thrives in a conducive environment. Study your hull for areas where rain may collect and cause frequent intervals of damp and dry. Where the hull meets the deck is a favorite, as are any corners where little puddles settle after rain or after boat washing. The constant drying/wetting encourages rust as no other action can.

For some reason, deck rust can only be found when on one's knees. If you can see it while standing, it has progressed farther than it should have. Get humble, with a screwdriver in hand, and probe gently in vulnerable areas where water will puddle. Often rust moves insidiously underneath a coat of paint that has become brittle and that has developed a crack too small for the eye to see but one that lets in air and water nonetheless. The rust creeps under the perfect looking paint, happily rusting your deck undetected until exposed by your searching screwdriver.

A properly prepared and painted deck provides the best rust protection. One surprising solution was passed on to me by Nick de Vries, a retired Dutch jet fighter pilot and acrobatic team captain who built his own large and elegant barge home. He treats the bare metal before the first coat of paint. First he brushes the bare steel with used oil--the type you extract from an engine oil change. *"Let that sit for a number of days"*, he said, quoting the old bargers, *"and then apply a good quality oil-based paint."*

To handle rust spots after sanding, I apply "Owatrol". It chemically changes the molecular structure, I am told, to convert rust into paint. I also mix some Owatrol into the primer and the finish coat as additional rust prevention.

For more information: Owachem B.V., Oosthavenkade 57, 3134 NX Vlaardingen, The Netherlands.

Top quality paint is very important. Metal expands and contracts due to changes in temperature. It is important that the paint remain flexible enough to withstand these changes without peeling or cracking from brittleness.

Some of the best paint in the world--"Epiphanes"--is made in Holland. Available throughout the world, it is worth the modest extra cost to keep your barge looking good. More importantly, it will help keep the steel well protected from the ravages of the ever waiting water/air combination that constantly tries to make rust of your steel.

When it comes to hulls, perhaps the most obvious hull rust occurs at the spot where someone has scraped against a lock wall. The protective layer of paint is left on the concrete wall, soon to be replaced by that corrosive light red substance.

I like to keep a small paint brush always at the ready, immersed in a bottle of water--a trick I learned from a savvy old Dutchman. The water keeps the air away from the bristles so they cannot become dry and brittle, despite repeated usings. Soon after the inevitable meeting of hull against concrete, I sand the spot and apply "Owatrol". After a few hours, I use one brush to apply primer, wait a day and use another brush to put on the finish coat. The hull is protected and so is my pride. My sin is only a memory.

Less obvious deterioration of the hull occurs from rusting along the waterline. The principle, you see, is the same. This is the area of the hull that is constantly exposed alternatingly to water and air.

With an old barge, as most are, the hull's weakest points are two: the waterline when she was empty (close to the turn of the bilge) and the waterline when she was fully loaded. If your barge is properly ballasted, the new waterline is probably somewhere in between the old waterlines, providing a "fresh" waterline that has yet to be tried by the constant wash of air and water. In a way, the new waterline gives your barge new life, since both the empty and loaded waterlines are now moved to relatively protected positions well above or well below the water. Fully immersed sections of the hull are not very susceptible to rust.

I noted earlier that Klaus, our experienced marine welder, told me that rusting of the hull on a barge built around the turn of the century is not a serious problem because "*the rust is almost all out*". Those components within the steel likely to rust have already done so and the rate of rusting slows considerably with age. A stronger old barge has fewer aging problems, evidently, than an equally strong new barge. We humans should be so fortunate!

If, however, time and rust have worn the thickness of steel below acceptable minimums, the fix is relatively easy and inexpensive: weld on a new sheet of steel. Good barge surveyors measure the thickness of the hull, which should ideally be a minimum of 4 millimeters. If an area of hull dips frequently into the 3 millimeter range, it is time to consider sheet steel.

Surveyors use one of two devices to measure hull thickness. The old fashioned way is to drill at selected spots. The holes of course are welded shut afterward. The second, a cheaper and more modern way, uses an electronic device that provides a thickness readout. Although generally considered reliable, these instruments are still controversial in some quarters.

Once assured of adequate hull thickness, follow the basic principle for rust prevention--isolate the hull from the elements. With barges, this is done with tar, a dirty job that is usually repeated every four years. Tar is not as antifouling as modern paints, but it is much cheaper and does the job for the mighty behemoths cruising the Rhine, so you may be assured it will do the job for you as well. Be sure to have the job bid ahead of time and use a commercial barge yard rather than a yacht yard. The price is much less.

Properly accomplished, tarring below the waterline and painting above it will prevent contact between steel and oxygen, and, to the extent successful, will lick the problem. If you are the particularly fastidious type, you can add an additional layer of protection topsides by waxing the hull. But I guarantee that "*energetic*" and "*persistent*" must be added to "*fastidious*". A barge becomes a huge amount of real estate when one starts polishing!

We Americans, with our preoccupation with fiberglass, often have uneasy feelings about electrolysis and corrosion associated with steel. It may give some comfort to know that, operating as they do in a fresh water environment, Europeans who have worked with steel barges as a livelihood for generations just gave me a patient quizzical look when I asked about electrolytic or galvanic corrosion on steel barges.

To protect the hull, the principle is simple. Avoid contact between steel and the air/water combination. Because one cannot avoid either water or air, check frequently the areas on the barge where those three are prone to have frequent contact and make sure your paint defenses are good.

TYPES OF STEERING

Rudders are made from one of two substances: wood or steel. They are controlled by one of four types of steering: chain, cable, shaft and gears, or hydraulics.

Unless yours is a special type sailing barge like a "*skutsje*" or something similar, steel is definitely a stronger and more preferred material for the rudder. It is strong and won't splinter or rot. If the barge you are in love with has a wood rudder, it may be fine. Just be aware that it needs to be thoroughly inspected by a knowledgeable professional and maintained properly. The safest bet, though, is steel.

Barge rudders are attached to the aft end of the hull, generally hung onto the hull (or skeg) by pins on the leading edge of the rudder (called pintles) inserted into round pipe-like receptacles on the skeg (called gudgeons). What you call them doesn't matter. Their strength and location do matter. Because the pintles are usually at the leading edge of the rudder, it is highly unbalanced and difficult to turn against the thrust of the propeller. If there is any way to balance the rudder by extending any part of it forward of the pintles--or moving the pintles aft to near the mid-point of the rudder--it will be much easier to steer. The thrusting water will push against both the leading and trailing edges of the rudder. Imagine how a seesaw with children of equal weight on both ends is much easier to operate than one with a child on only one end.

In addition to noting how a rudder is balanced and whether it is wood or steel, check the method of steerage. Any of the types will do, as long as they are in good condition. The oldest and strongest is chain. The chain is normally led through a series of pulleys, or blocks, as it snakes from the steering wheel to the rudder. It is susceptible to jamming by any foreign object (especially mislaid mooring lines) at the turning blocks and will also be a greasy inconvenience to polished shoes that trip on its exposed portions. Usually straight runs are housed in secured steel pipe. Proper tension is important to ease of handling--a phrase used advisedly--and there normally is a threaded tension adjuster inserted in the chain which should be checked regularly. Should the threaded rod unscrew itself, you will suddenly have no steerage!

Of the four steering methods, chain is the least user friendly. One can use this method as a body building exercise. Nevertheless, knowledgeable bargers have used chain for generations. If you watch them, note that they idle the engine before they turn the wheel so as to reduce the thrust of the water against the rudder, and consequently the amount of pressure the wheel must resist. Conversely, when they straighten out after a turn, they will goose the engine to let prop thrust help push the rudder back amidships.

Chain drive steering illustrates a major maxim of barge handling--it is quite simple once a person learns to work *with* the barge, allowing its forces to make life simpler and easier. Don't expect "the feel" to come too quickly. It just takes a little time and a lot of attention to what the barge is saying. Hopefully, this book will speed the learning curve a bit. Just give it time. Listen to your barge. Feel it.

A cable steering system--actually a combination of chain and cable with chain on the steering wheel cogs and cable for the runs--has less drag, less weight, and consequently usually steers a bit more easily. It is not quite as strong but is less susceptible to jamming by errant mooring lines.

A shaft and gear steering system normally is used when the pilothouse is set further aft and the run between the wheel and rudder is not very long. These have the least friction. If properly geared they are both strong and relatively simple. Check the gear alignment and keep the gears and shaft holders lubricated with a heavy grease.

Hydraulic steerage is the most modern and user friendly system available. It is also quite expensive and often requires an engine-mounted pump with adequate power to counter the thrust against the rudder. As with most modern systems, maintenance is critically important, in this case of the pump, the oil and the rubber hoses. The cost of failure of any part can be very damaging. Overall, hydraulics are more complex and expensive, but much easier to use.

Any of these systems are adequate as long as they are stout and that good maintenance and proper barge handling techniques are practiced. The simplest is the strongest, the complex is easiest and most expensive.

FENDERS

When tons of steel meet solid concrete, strong fenders are important. We started out with socially acceptable polyurethane tube fenders--standard sport boat fenders. Though oversized, they were quickly squashed by our 60 tons, and lasted but a few weeks. Then we did like some big barges do--we experimented with blocks of wood. Their chief advantage is that, when broken, they float and don't foul the lock gates.

Wood works well but it has **no** cushion when steel meets concrete. You really clunk.

Tires work wonderfully but are officially banned in all countries, though enforcement varies. Too often the line between tire and boat breaks under tension and the tire sinks to the bottom. Sooner or later it gets stuck between the lock gates, prevents a closing seal and makes the lock useless until the tire is removed.

We found one solution: we put inflated tubes in the tires. Should the tire lanyard break, the tire floats. We also painted the tires and tubes white. They look more attractive and lockkeepers can quickly see the inflated tubes on the inside of the tires, which moderates their concern about sinking tires. Since we improvised this, we have had few objections from lockkeepers. (Like bureaucrats, there are always a few letter-of-the-law sticklers.) Because European tire dealers have to pay the equivalent of about $1 for each tire needing disposal, they are only too happy to have you relieve them of a few, and may even give you some old inner tubes at the same time. Otherwise you may have to pay a bit for the inner tubes, which our kids--and grown up kids--found handy for swimming (and person overboard use, in case it was necessary, which in our case, fortunately, never was). Many European cars use smaller tires that make fenders more user friendly.

We used two tires the size one would expect on a wheel barrow as portable fenders. Believe me, having one of these at both bow and stern can come in very handy. No matter how carefully we planned our moorings in locks or against walls, something unexpected occurred more often than not and hull and wall made contact where we hadn't anticipated. Alert crew can insert fenders to cushion the contact. These portable fenders save time that would otherwise be spent painting nicks and scratches.

To extend the life of tire lanyards, use a heavy duty drill and knife to pierce two holes about six inches apart in the tire tread. Loop the lanyard through the holes so the lanyard does not wear against either the boat or the lock. A friend used another technique--he used chain as a lanyard to install his white tire fenders permanently.

Before painting the tire, I suggest you clean it thoroughly. An old tire will absorb paint somewhat like a sponge, leaving a dishwater blond look to the tire despite an additional coat. To my surprise, latex paint holds up better than oil based. With newer, clean tires, a couple coats should produce a nice finish.

If the fenders scrape hard against a mossy, gunky lock wall, clean the fender before it dries to make the job easier. We were surprised at how good looking our painted tires were, considering their heavy duty use.

Your ship looks sharper if fenders don't drag in the water while underway. A barge looks best without fenders, of course, and in Holland we only put fenders out when they were needed for locks or mooring. In France, the locks are so frequent that we left them out.

The ultimate fender is a sausage shaped woven rope affair placed horizontally just above the waterline. It also has an ultimate price.

We finally came upon our ultimate affordable solution when it came time to recycle old mooring lines. We made our own rope fenders. They work the best yet!

To make these, cut off the loop end of the old mooring line with about four feet attached to the loop. Set it aside for a moment. Then loop the old mooring line like a cowboy would, except maybe a slightly smaller loop--about 18 inches in diameter. Loop it five or six times; you may vary it depending upon the desired thickness of the fender. When you have sufficient line for your fender, cut it. It now looks like a really limp Cheerio. Now, using smaller line wrapped at six inch intervals, convert the looped line into a tight sausage about six inches in diameter. Finally, take the loop end of the old mooring line set aside earlier, insert it through the top of the Cheerio hole of the sausage and draw the other end of the loop line through itself. Bingo! A very serviceable fender at the right price.

Think carefully about fender placement. Anticipate where the hull may bump most often and place the fenders accordingly as shock absorbers. A little cruising experience will quickly aid accurate placement. On each side we placed two fenders strategically along the turn of the hull by the bow, another roughly amidships, and a fourth at the turn of the hull aft.

DINGHIES

Dinghies are useful for lakes. If you are largely confined to canals, don't bother. Holland and Scandinavia have the most lakes. If you plan to cruise significantly there, the dinghy is a good investment for getting around when anchored. Anytime you transit a significant body of water where chop may develop--anathema to barges--the dinghy becomes a prudent lifesaving device as well. But on the canals the nearest lifesaving device is usually within about ten feet: the canal bank. On the canal the dinghy becomes a superfluous bit of deck clutter.

ELECTRONICS

This is the brief and simple section. You really don't need any electronics on a recreational barge. Given the American penchant for gadgetry, this may be difficult to accept; but true. That is not to say, however, that certain equipment may not come in handy. For those of you who need a microchip nearby to feel complete, here are some considerations:

VHF. The "*Marifoon*" as the Dutch call it, can be useful for ship to ship communication, to contact bridge and lock controllers, and occasionally for telephone conversations. It is most useful in Holland and Germany, where many lockmasters may be called on VHF to alert them to your imminent arrival. We found, however, that few lockmasters speak English and it takes a strong mastery of the local language to converse successfully, given their generally clipped dialect on the radio. Besides, the big locks with VHF are normally on a regular cycle you need to fit into. Though we used the VHF at first, we doubt it gained us much and quit before long. The smaller locks in Belgium and France have no VHF, so its only use there is for occasional conversations with other barges. If you know the language, it is helpful. In Holland and the Scandinavian countries, enough bargers speak English to make it useful even if you don't know the local tongue.

Holland also has an efficient system of hourly broadcasts of the call signs of those boats having long distance telephone calls standing by for contact, and in theory France does too, though it is quite complex and, given France's uneven terrain and the general 24 mile limit to VHF communications, it is less practical there. Frankly, we did not rely on VHF for emergency communications from home. Instead, we telephoned AT&T or another US carrier to check with family and friends back home on a regular basis. (Some credit card companies offer a free message service which you may call collect from around the world to check for messages. For more on this, see the section on Telephone in Chapter 9, *Cruising Considerations*.)

Depthsounder. Useless. As a sailor who cruises in the Pacific Northwest where rocks suddenly erupt from deep waters, I consider the depthsounder the most important component after the rudder. It wasn't long, however, before I realized that the canal depths were always four to eight feet and running aground did not have the serious consequences of grounding on rocks in the San Juan Islands. It just meant I was oozing into mud, from which I could ordinarily unooze. If you are the curious type who wants to know whether you have six feet or six inches under you in a given canal--though there is nothing useful you can do with that information--then get the depthsounder. Otherwise, save your money.

Knotmeter. See above under "Depthsounder". Another useless piece of gear. The Canal charts are so detailed that it is easy to mark one's position and use time and distance to calculate speed.

Calculator. Now there is a useful electronic instrument aboard a barge! If you must have electronics, spend $5 for a calculator! It is handy to figure speed, fuel consumption rates, and estimated times of arrival at the next alluring village, to say nothing of currency conversion and budgeting.

Bowthruster. See Chapter 3, *Stopping and Turning*, and Chapter 10, *How to Buy a Barge*.

Needless to say, if you need a GPS, you shouldn't be aboard a barge! The chart will indicate that you are 1100 meters from the next village and 990 meters from the next garbage can. It even numbers the locks. (And there are no coordinates on canal charts!)

Radar is used only by the big barges that run day and night and in fog on the river. Recreational bargers should never run at night. So leave the radar on the boat back home.

A timepiece is handy to announce lunch and project arrival times, but I found that my barging lifestyle ethic required that I give my wristwatch a rest. I referred to the clock only for meals and to record the beginning and the end of the cruising day. Note, however, it did not dictate our schedule, only recorded it. We began when we felt like it and stopped at whatever seemed like a "nice spot".

There really aren't any other electronics that you should even consider, much less need. After all, barging brings one back to the basics.

Look for strength and durability in equipment: reliable engine, solid hull, strong rudder with a dependable steering system and minimal electronics. Maintain the equipment well, keep the rust off the hull, change the oil often, relax and enjoy yourself.

Chapter 9

CRUISING CONSIDERATIONS

You have read the preceding chapters, arranged for the barge, and are ready to cruise the canals. Here are a few tips that may help along the way, from where to buy fuel to moorage and lock fees, charts, licensing, rules of the road, telephones, and what to do if a person falls overboard.

FUEL

Fuel costs more in Europe. It is a culture shock upon arrival, and you may as well get used to it. Europeans pay higher fuel taxes, which accounts for part of the increased cost. Plus, their source is more expensive. Europe is nearly 100% dependent upon the Mideast for fossil fuels, whereas we in the United States have a greater domestic supply. So they not only pay more to purchase it, they must pay to transport it from the Mideast to the continent as well.

Within Europe, however, there are significant differences in the price you must pay, as of this writing. Varying taxes on barge fuel account for most price differences. Whereas nearly all countries have significant road taxes on automotive and truck fuels, some reduce or eliminate the tax for waterborne craft.

The incremental moves toward a united Europe may reduce or even end the variances in barge fuel rates from country to country. As I write, however, the best barge fuel rates are in Belgium. Most commercial bargers fuel up in Belgium as they head south into the significantly more expensive France. After Belgium, Holland and Luxembourg have the next cheapest diesel rates (although one can only access Luxembourg along the Mosel River), followed by France and finally Germany.

As an example, on our cruise in 1990 and 1991, we paid the equivalent of $.30/liter in Belgium (about $1.15/gallon), $.40/liter in Holland, the same in Luxembourg, $.61/liter in France, and $.75/liter in Germany.

Whenever possible, buy fuel where the commercial bargers do. Often the price can be negotiated: the more purchased the less the cost per liter (a gallon equals about 3.8 liters). I suspect the same fuel stop in Belgium near the French border may well charge less for barges heading north than for those heading south into France. Because the next fueling station (France) is twice the price, one's bargaining position heading south is seriously jeopardized. In addition, we did not find any competition in the border towns, which further complicated our position. I never did this little maneuver, but I suspect it may help price-wise to pass by the establishment when heading south, then do a U-turn so it appears you are heading north. It may also pay to top off fuel at the second to the last stop before the French border, where one's options are a bit greater.

Be prepared to pay cash for fuel. Credit cards may be accepted at some Dutch (MasterCard) and French (Visa) fuel stops, but most prefer cash, especially if the price is negotiable.

Generally, we found no difference in the quality of the fuel from country to country, except in the East Bloc which had just been emancipated when we were there. Our rental car, for instance, immediately pinged, and lost both power and fuel mileage when we filled our tank in the then Czechoslovakia in 1991.

Taxes are significantly lower on home heating fuel than on motor fuel, even though, other than some additives, it is essentially the same product. You are officially required to have a separate tank aboard for home heating diesel. To further complicate matters, both France and Germany (and possibly other countries), put a red pigment in the home heating fuel to differentiate it from white road fuel. Rumor had it that police and customs officials would sometimes draw a sample from your motor fuel tank. If it contained any red pigment, substantial fines could ensue. We were even told that the Germans so constructed their home heating fuel mixture that burning it in a diesel motor caused the exhaust to turn red! We found that to be a baseless rumor however, when we were cruising Germany's Neckar River in the fall and winter and heated our barge with a diesel fired circulating hot water boiler. Because our boiler draws fuel directly from the engine fuel tank, we had no way to separate the fuels. After calculating roughly how much motor fuel we had used to heat our barge, we asked the local furnace oil man to bring his truck and replenish our tanks with an equivalent amount of home heating fuel. It cost about .70DM($.45) per liter compared to 1.20DM($.75) per liter for motor fuel. There was no change in the color of the exhaust.

An English boater we met reported that for insurance in France he purchased motor fuel periodically, retaining the receipts to show in case of inspection. Others report random "color" inspections and stiff fines. Once red fuel is in the tank, it takes many fillings to dilute it out.

A note of caution on home heating fuel during the winter: it becomes "jellied" at -4 degrees Celsius--not that far below freezing, in contrast to motor fuel which is fortified to stay liquid to far colder temperatures. By mixing the two fuels in Germany, we avoided engine problems.

Because commercial barges use fuel to produce taxable income, they are exempt from paying the VAT (Value Added Tax) on fuel. Not so recreational boats. Items for export, however, are exempt from the VAT, depending upon the circumstances and providing the purchase is large enough. In some cases, since ours was an American registered vessel (even though it was a Dutch barge), we were able to get our 18.5% VAT refunded to us by the diesel supplier. We registered the vessel at the American Consulate (we did ours in Amsterdam), kept the receipt for the VAT paid (we did have to first pay the VAT and then hope for a refund), had the receipt stamped by the customs official as we crossed the border, and mailed the stamped receipt to the fuel dealer in the hope that he would deposit the VAT refund in the Dutch Bank account whose number we enclosed. The refund isn't guaranteed, of course, as we found out when some customs people stamped the receipts and others refused.

Don't allow me to confuse the issue. The best tactic when buying diesel fuel in a given country is to ask the bargers for their recommendation on where the best price is. When transiting countries, try to fill up in Belgium.

Besides motor fuel, propane (stove and hot water) is the other fuel most commonly purchased. It generally comes in what we would call 5 gallon cans. In Holland, France, and Belgium, empty cans are exchanged for full ones. Only in Germany do they refill containers as they do in the US.

The only problem we encountered with exchanging propane containers is that, like in many other matters, France has its own ways and does not necessarily accept those of others. We were told in Holland, for instance, that the Esso propane containers we used there were interchangeable throughout the continent. And although we did manage to cajole an occasional propane dealer in Belgium and France into accepting our Esso cans, the general rule in France was "*Non* ". Not only would they not accept cans from another country, they did not want to accept cans from another propane company, even if it was also French! European unity may standardize propane containers someday, but the little French villages along the canals will probably be the last to know.

Whereas in Holland many residents heat with cheap and plentiful natural gas, and Belgium is built on a giant coal field, in France many homes are heated with bottled propane gas. Consequently, bargers purchase propane in Holland and Belgium primarily from canal side service stations or service barges; but in France, the propane is carried by all of the large supermarkets, usually at their on site gas station.

Prices for propane are far more consistent than for motor fuel. A five gallon refill, based on an exchange rate of roughly 2 Dutch guilders or 5.5 French francs to the US dollar, costs about $17. One tank lasted us three weeks, which supplied us with "on demand" domestic hot water and cooking fuel for our family of six.

Our bottom line recommendation on propane is this: carry several containers. If France is on the itinerary, have at least one French tank before arriving or you may have to purchase one.

TRANSPORTATION

In addition to your moving waterfront home, there are several forms of transportation in Europe.

Public transportation, particularly trains and buses in Holland, and trains in France, will take you virtually anywhere. They are not inexpensive, but they have frequent departures.

With planks hewn by a German sawmill, we load our Austin "Mini" the first time. It now takes about five minutes.

We found bicycles to be a wonderful means of exploring cities and transporting goods. They carried groceries on racks and in bags, and even hauled lumber, using a forward and aft bicycle. Folding bicycles (like "Dahon") take minimal space. Standard bicycles allow you to travel longer distances in comfort. Some prefer mopeds.

Cars can be handy, but only if you can take it aboard. Otherwise, a car becomes a merciless hassle. Rental cars for special occasions are a good option. They are inexpensive, except in France. In all cases, make rental car reservations through your travel agent in the States, even if you call them from Europe--you can save up to 50%. Check the "Van Wijk" agency in Holland and Belgium. They offer Hertz cars at discount prices.

MOORING FEES

There is never a charge for tying to a rural canal bank. But mooring inside a city can be different, and the rates vary widely.

Dutch towns often charge about a guilder ($.65) per meter (3 feet+) of boat length, more if moored in a private marina. Being on a budget, we often moored during the day inside the city, enjoyed the sights, and then tied up for the night by some quiet grassy bank outside town. Yet, some cities like Kampen and Deventer, charged nothing. In fact, we stayed for several days north of the Ij River in Amsterdam for no fee whatever.

I do not recall that we were ever charged for mooring in Belgium, though one needs to be selective about where to moor in that country.

The French national government, I am told, provided grants to canal side villages to construct little mooring walls and marinas to attract passing boaters. Many are complete with showers, water, and even electricity. Originally, no one charged for these services. Increasingly, however, village budgeteers see the potential for a revenue source and, in 1991, a few were beginning to charge modest 10FF to 25FF fees per boat ($2 to $5) for moorage. I suspect the practice will spread as the mayors convene in conferences and chat about how to raise more revenue.

Mooring in Paris can be quite expensive at the downtown Arsenal marina (20FF[$4]+ per meter), not far from Notre Dame; but there is no charge for rafting between the Isle de France and the bank, just downstream from the Eiffel Tower.

Though not ordinarily possible in Paris, one can tie to city walls in many larger cities without incurring a charge.

We found the German marinas charged about one DM ($.70) per meter along the Rhine. Because of the Rhine's current, recreational barges seldom tie to a city wall along this mighty undammed river, seeking refuge either in one of the off-channel marinas or anchorages in riverside inlets.

The Neckar River communities delightfully welcomed to us and no city charged us for the privilege of tying to their city wall. The Mosel, on the other hand, is a beautiful lady who knows it, and likes to be paid for the privilege of holding her hand. The picturesque city of Cochem, for instance, charges a mark a meter, though truthfully it is a small price to pay to lie amid her splendor.

Overall, one has to marvel at how inexpensive fees really are, considering the investment made in constructing and maintaining these magnificent waterways throughout the continent.

CHARTS

France and Holland produce wonderful canal charts. Both make them for Belgium as well. Germany has commercial barge charts and some nice recreational guides but they are not up to the Dutch and French standards and much more difficult to procure.

Both the Dutch and French charts are wonderfully detailed, containing every bit of imaginable helpful information. The canal system of the two countries is divided into sections, and a given chart will cover a particular section. France has two main chart publishers. They vary a bit in style but are priced similarly. Get whichever suits your personal preference (though not all waterways have charts made by both companies).

Holland has so many spider web patterned canals that they make canal charts that fold like American road maps. Opened and spread, they show a region with all the canals going this way and that. In the few areas where the waterway is a single one, like the Maas River, they bind it in a tall narrow booklet. Some 18 charts cover the waterways of The Netherlands. Most cost about 20Dfl (Dutch Guilders, about $13) and are available from the Dutch super equivalent of the AAA called ANWB (pronounced "*ah-en-vay-bay*"). This agency provides a host of services from tours to automobile safety equipment to marine insurance.

Upon request, the ANWB will supply a sheet listing the English version of the chart symbols ("*Verklaring*"). I highly recommend you memorize them. The charts themselves show such details as church steeples, canal depths, clearance height of bridges, and dimensions of all locks. Scales vary from 1:25,000 to 1:50,000.

The ANWB also publishes two thick little books, one of which, the inland water regulations, is required to be aboard your vessel--even though written in Dutch. We complied. Why ruffle official feathers unnecessarily? The more useful of the two is the Almanac, published yearly, which provides much useful information. The most helpful for the touring English speaker is the schedule for bridge and lock operation. Minor locks and bridges are frequently closed on Sundays, at noon, and at a given evening hour. There are different schedules for spring, fall, and summer. Though this book also is in the native tongue, the Dutch alphabetize just as we do, so it is not difficult to find the bridge or lock you have in mind. Hours are expressed using a 24 hour military-like clock. You may also find, as we did, that of all the main European languages, Dutch is most like English. Before long we could decipher enough of the written--and spoken--words to get along decently well, even if we had to strain to roll our Rs and form our Gs down by our tonsils.

The nineteen plus French canal charts do not spread out like Dutch waterway charts and American road maps. Rather, because French canals spread more like fingers and less like spider webs, the charts follow a particular canal. They are bound like a book with the canal running down the middle of each page from top to bottom. Descriptions and symbols are in English and German, as well as, of course, French. (Our observation is that most canaliers on the French waterways are not French at all, but Germans, Swiss, and Dutchmen). Just when one cannot imagine a more detailed chart than that which the Dutch produce, the French do. Little symbols even show the locations of bakeries, supermarkets, telephones, and even garbage cans!

At the end of each French chartbook is a tidy Michelin-guide type tourist summary highlighting attractions along the canal.

The most common French charts cost up to 120FF($25) each and are produced by *Editions Cartographiques Maritimes*, 7 Quai Gabriel Peri, 94340 Joinville le Pont. Be sure to get the "*Itineraires Fluviaux*" which contains a map showing all the waterways of France and Belgium, as well as a critically important chart symbol guide, also written in the three languages.

The German charts have an entirely different character and are much more difficult to obtain, probably because cruising the German rivers recreationally is not as common as in France, Belgium, and Holland.

The German charts are of two types: recreational books and profes-sional barge charts. The former are small books, almost small enough to be called booklets, and are a combination guidebook/chartbook. The charts lack the detail of the Dutch and French charts but do provide the essentials--the location of the deep channels and where the locks and cit-ies are. They are all written in German, though their real value lies in the sketched waterway charts and symbols.

The professional German charts are intended for the primary water-ways. The one we saw covered the Rhine and the Mosel. Available in very large (2' x 3') renditions, or a more compact booklet, they provide significantly more detail than do the recreational versions.

The recreational books are available from the relatively obscure Ger-man chandleries and the professional versions from German barge sup-pliers. We found them nearly impossible to obtain outside Germany, so we suggest writing ahead to obtain them.

Only the benevolent hospitality of a trusting German boater enabled us to enter Germany with a suitable chart of the great Rhine River. Having failed to find German charts in chandleries along our cruising routes through Holland, Belgium, and France, I was near panic when we arrived in the French/German border city of Strasbourg, about to enter the mighty revered Rhine River with no chart other than a road map!

I scoured Strasbourg in desperation. I climbed staircases in the many storied grand French government buildings, and was referred from one level of bureaucracy to another. All to no avail. It seemed the French perceived that the world ended at the French border.

Finally, the evening before our scheduled entry into the great river, I helped two German recreational power boaters looking for moorage (scarce in Strasbourg) tie alongside our barge. A friendly chat ensued, and we were soon invited aboard. I lost no time seeking counsel on the River Rhine, explaining my "sans chart" predicament and asking advice on where to procure one. My newly found non-English speaking German friend promptly produced his own small version of the professional chartbook and told me to use it as long as needed. I could mail it to him when I was finished, he said. Even when I protested that it might be six months before we left the German rivers, he insisted. He knew the River by heart and did not require the chartbook, he said. We mailed it back to him the following spring, forever impressed with the camaraderie among waterfolk and his generosity. Once I studied it and entered the Rhine, I concluded that I would never want to enter without a chart. In the words of the commercial, *"don't leave home without it."*

Later, while visiting in Holland at New Years, a Dutch friend (Arend Bonsink, the mechanic who installed our engine) dashed upstairs and loaned us a singed professional chartbook to the Rhine and Mosel Rivers. He had purchased a burned out boat to reconstruct and this had been among its charred contents. I used it to good advantage. Only on the Neckar did I have to resort to the guidebooks, which are also produced for the Main and the beautiful but short River Lahn.

LICENSING

There are two important rules about licensing in the highly regulated continent we call Europe. First, all skippers need to be licensed. Second, some nations pretty much respect the licensing laws of the skipper's country of origin. Knowing only the first rule can make the cruise seem impossible. Knowing the latter rescues it.

All the countries we cruised require licensing of professional pilots, as does the United States. However, Germany, Holland, and most recently France also require licensing of recreational skippers; in the case of Holland and France, of vessels 15 meters (49 feet) and longer. The Dutch, which passed the law in 1992, unfortunately have neither the regulations nor the tests in anything but the Dutch language. I suspect, however, that what happened to us in Germany may also occur in Holland. In fact, the Dutch recently decided to accept some licensing levels from the UK for various bodies of water. I am told the Dutch also accept the French license.

The French license law, reportedly passed in 1994, requires a physical by a French doctor, a passing score on the written exam, and successful transit through a lock and back again with the inspector on board. The written exam consists largely of identifying chart symbols. Not many people have experience with this exam at this writing, nor the degree of enforcement.

The French have a different attitude toward government than we Americans. They have mixed emotions--sometimes reverent as if Napoleon were the government, other times they act as if the 1789 rebellion against all institutions of society is about to be re-enacted. Napoleon wins out most of the time, though. The French Parliament seems to enact laws just in case the esteemed bureaucracy may decide to reach into its tool box of laws and apply it if needed. It's too early to see what the fate of the French licensing law will be, though it seems to be gaining some momentum. By not applying to boats under 15 meters it exempts the self-drive penichettes. In my experience, these were the ones more often guilty of excessive speed, inappropriately caused wakes, and bank erosion.

As I indicated briefly in Chapter 7, the German water police ("*Wassershutzpolizei*") are charged with enforcing regulations along the rivers. The Germans believe in instructed competence so firmly, says our American friend living in Germany, that they send prospective fishermen seeking licenses to a six week school capped by a mind-breaking exam. The resulting license enables one to catch but one type of fish, and only on a specific river. So we should not have been surprised when a German skipper told us that recreational skipper licenses are limited in scope: special licenses for a given size of boat, and only for a given stretch of river. A German may have a license for the Mosel for a 50 foot boat, but he cannot do the Rhine. That takes a separate school and a separate exam.

The German water police, however, allowed us to continue on all three rivers (Neckar, Rhine, and Mosel) because we met the requirements of our own country to navigate inland waterways as recreational boaters--which is no requirement at all, thanks to the great American penchant for individual liberty. But our national standard is honored, thankfully, by the Germans.

Nonetheless, hanging by a legal thread can be precarious. Better that they have faith in your ability. The more paper evidence you have to demonstrate competence--diplomas from boating schools, US Coast Guard licenses, personal boating logs, photos of boats you have owned or chartered, letters attesting to your competence--all will make your visit smoother.

Beyond licensing, however, is the basic issue of competence and the respect for the laws and regulations of the host country. Foreigners are bound to judge us as a people based on what they observe in us as individuals. Like it or not, each of us is an ambassador. Knowledge of local customs and regulations demonstrates respect for the host country and, more importantly, assures the safety of boat and crew. The most important of these safety standards are the Rules of the Road.

RULES OF THE ROAD

European rules of the road conform to international standards and are neither difficult nor complicated. But, as understanding road signs is essential before one drives a car, they are absolutely mandatory to know. The symbols on the inside covers of this book are those I consider the most important for the waterways. Study them, review them, memorize them. They need to become second nature. One does not have time to consult the card when confronted by a barge rounding a river curve giving two short blasts on his horn as he bears down on you.

BLUE FLAGGING

We had just purchased our barge, fitted the new engine, and embarked on our European cruise. At our first stop in the Dutch city of Zwolle, we met Mr. Vander Veen, whose boat was next to ours on the city mooring wall. As we visited together, I was intrigued to learn he was a retired instructor at a Dutch "barge skipper's school". The next morning I asked his advice.

"*If there were one important item I should know*," I asked, "*what would that be?*" "*I'm glad you asked*," he replied. "*I couldn't get to sleep last night. I kept seeing you colliding with another barge on the river.*"

Then he explained the blue flag rule. (See also chapters 6 and 7.) After 3,000 miles of cruising, I would agree with my friend Mr. Vander Veen. The "blue flag" rule is indeed the most critical.

Actually, it is very simple. A vessel over 20 meters may signal oncoming water traffic that it will move from the normal right hand side of the channel (just like driving one's car), to the **left** hand side of the channel (just like driving one's car in England). Oncoming vessels so equipped will acknowledge by flying their own blue flag in response.

And so, for an instant, one is transported figuratively to England, where all drive the left hand side. A moment later, a barge without a blue flag appears and the roles are instantly reversed, back to normal right hand traffic patterns.

The reason for the blue flag rule is a good one. The deepest water and the fastest current lie on the outside of a river's curve. A barge laboring upstream can save both distance and time by cutting the corner on a curve that swerves to the left. By negotiating the inside of the curve, the upstreaming barge makes faster speed over ground in the slower current, and cuts the distance traveled as well. Especially along the strongly currented rivers like the Rhine, which run free of dams and locks, this becomes an essential technique for upstream bound barges.

What I call a blue "flag" really is not a flag at all. It actually is a one meter (a little more than a yard) square that looks like a piece of cardboard with little holes drilled in it. The hardly visible holes let air through in windy conditions. The blue field is bordered by a white frame. In the center of the square is a flashing white light, useful especially at night when these mighty monsters still roam the rivers' ways (and all recreational barges should be securely moored). The blue "flag" is affixed to the starboard side of the barge pilothouse and when not employed, lies flat on a rotating axis. When the barge skipper wishes to "blue flag", he reaches up and flips a lever which springs the square flag from horizontal to vertical, and starts the center light flashing.

Recreational barges that cruise only on canals may seldom if ever encounter a commercial barge flying a blue flag. But they are very common on rivers.

As we were swept down the mighty current of Germany's Rhine River, Mr. Vander Veen's collision nightmare was always in the back of my mind. We grabbed for binoculars whenever we saw a barge emerge from around a bend. We knew as we headed downstream that if the river curve in front of us bore away to our right, most likely any barge we met would be blue flagging in order to gain the inside of the curve, away from the deepest, swiftest current. (Forget the old adage that "*still waters run deep*". In our experience, the opposite is true.)

On one Rhine occasion, I observed to my wife Marlene that commercial barges acted like high school girls going to the bathroom--it seems they just can't go alone. We always met them in groups. One time we met a group of five. Two were blue flagging, with one blue flagger passing the other blue flagger. The other three were not blue flagging, and one of them was passing the other two. Given the blue flagging rule, we had to run the chute between them, with two on our left and three on our right. I confess my knuckles were a bit on the white side as I looked up at the huge black steel hulks on either side of our seemingly tiny boat at what felt like 100 miles an hour. I mentally tipped my hat to Mr. Vander Veen as I emerged unscathed through the pack.

RED RIGHT RETURNING TO THE HARBOR

This is one of the first ditties learned by aspiring salt water navigators. Always leave the red buoy to the right hand side when returning to the harbor.

The same rule applies on the rivers. The harbor happens to be at the opposite end--at the mouth of the river. But one can use the ditty just the same. Whenever traveling downstream, a barge of course is always heading toward the harbor. And when heading downstream toward the harbor, the buoys should always be kept to the right--or starboard--of the barge.

Of course, that also means when heading **downstream**, the green buoys will be to port.

When heading **upstream**, reverse the buoys since the barge is now heading away from the harbor. Now, it's green buoys to starboard, red to port. This may seem simple--and it is. But imagine being carried rapidly downstream by a boisterous river current. Suddenly you see a red buoy on the left half of the river channel! With no time for research and the fate of your ship possibly at stake, you run a quick mental double check of the rule (yes I am heading downstream toward the harbor. Yes, the red needs to be on my right) before you steer toward the port shore to follow the deep channel marked out by the navigation officials, and thereby avoid losing the propeller to the shoal that juts out invisibly from the starboard bank.

BRIDGE SIGNS

I think every multi-span river bridge under which we cruised used the right of way signs to direct which span was one-way and which was two-way, and which was no way.

Upon rare occasion the chart conflicted with the actual signage on the bridge. In one case I recall, the chart for the Rhine showed different spans open than did the actual signs on the bridge. Slightly unnerved, I decided correctly to observe the posted rather than the charted signs.

One sign can cause confusion. A square "do not enter" sign with an arrow is posted on some bridge abutments. Does it mean "do not enter here and proceed in the direction of the arrow"? Or "do not enter where the arrow points"? It is the latter. The sign location does not matter. The area the arrow points to is the key to avoid.

The rest of the signs on the inside covers are also important, but less likely to cause confusion. I suggest you obtain a copy to post in the pilothouse for instant reference. The one shown is taken from the inside cover of the French "*Service de Navigation*" chart for its overall French canal map.

The best advice one can give on Rules of the Road comes in two words from Professor Vander Veen: "*Know them.*"

PERSON OVERBOARD DRILL

Those of you who are experienced boaters will say "*Of course, the old person overboard drill. Here it comes again. Throw the life ring. Appoint a pointer. Go back and get them.*"

Not so. The environment in the canal is very much different than the open water that so many of us are accustomed to.

If an adult falls overboard while cruising down a canal, they should swim (or walk on the bottom in some cases) to the side of the canal about ten feet away.

Usually, only if a child unable to swim falls overboard must one think conventionally about rescue. In such a case, the primary concern is the propeller. Remember that it sucks a great amount of water, so know where the overboard person is before engaging either forward or reverse with any significant thrust. Probably the best immediate reaction in case of overboard is to instinctively place the transmission in neutral. Then collect your thoughts and plan a course of action.

The closest you will come to conventional person overboard drill is on a very large canal or a river where the water may be deep, the current may be strong, and the banks are a fair distance.

The point is this: think it out ahead of time. What would you do right now if someone were to go overboard?

If headed upstream and a person fell overboard, the barge would need to stop and probably turn around.

If headed downstream, one must decide between a quick reverse to allow the current to bring the person alongside or turning upstream. Local conditions and the distance between the barge and the overboard person would dictate the best course. Again, it is useful to contemplate various conditions and pre-plan contingencies.

Before debarking, ensure sufficient Personal Flotation Devices (PFDs--commonly called lifejackets) are aboard, as well as life rings that can be tossed to the person overboard. On any river, any passenger who either cannot swim or has limited ability should definitely wear a PFD anytime they venture outside the cabin. In fact, it is a good idea for all passengers who venture on deck, even the good swimmers.

Aboard a barge, the biggest single danger of a person falling overboard occurs not on the canals or rivers, but within the confines of a lock. That is when crew are at the edge of the barge, leaning outboard to secure lines to bollards. As discussed in Chapter 2, the greatest danger for a person overboard is being crushed between the wall of the lock and the barge. That is another reason it is **so** important to know instinctively the torque of the propeller of the barge. Will reverse bring the hull against the person overboard, or away?

Stress this mental discipline: on **each** approach to a lock, mentally anticipate a crew overboard situation and think exactly what action you would take to prevent the crew from being crushed. That carefully planned anticipation defines one of the most important functions of a well-prepared skipper, who will hopefully never have to exercise that skill.

MONEY

Cash buys the fuel and food. European stores don't take dollars--US dollars, that is. There is serious talk of a "Eurodollar" called a "Euro" that is designed to be the universal currency for a united Europe. Agreements as of this writing call for its implementation in the leading European countries by 1999. Its success will make life much easier for the cruising canalier, who now must convert currency from country to country.

For visits of a month or less, I recommend that you exchange dollars for local currency at a local European bank. Check the exchange rates before departing for Europe (Wall Street Journal, in case a local newspaper does not carry them). Expect to pay about a 2% fee for exchanging money.

For those cruising for more than a month or two, a European bank account may be something to consider. To transfer money from the US, write a check or have money wired from your US bank to your European bank. The exchange rate is usually much better, especially if you follow the advice of a knowledgeable European banker. In our case, we used the directions of our Dutch ABN banker and obtained the best possible exchange rates, significantly better than the cash exchange rate at banks.

Exercise care in the process, however. We found we had to baby-sit our money, as in our case the wire worked at the speed of the Pony Express. It took three weeks and many long distance telephone calls to shepherd the money from our US bank to its New York exchange bank which transferred it to the Dutch ABN branch, also in New York, which then wired it to our local tiny ABN branch. The problem occurred with the US bank in New York, and our money simply sat on someone's desk while we waited patiently (well, not so patiently) to take possession of the barge we had purchased. During the delay, the exchange rate dipped, costing us an extra $800. Fortunately, all other transfers worked well. The smooth transfers were all by check.

Don't be surprised if the Dutch banker looks slightly amused at the sight of your check. They don't use them. Instead, they do virtually everything electronically, via interbank transfers. For instance, instead of sending a check to someone to pay a bill, you simply fill out a chit to your bank which instructs bank personnel to deposit X amount into the account of the person you are paying. There is no such thing as *"The check is in the mail"*.

France, on the other hand, resembles the US in bank procedures. They are a "normal" check writing country. Expect up to three weeks for the US check to clear into the French bank account, however.

When you select a bank, be sure to get one that has branches in small towns. Otherwise, it will be very difficult for you to draw cash from your account. In Holland, ABN/AMRO is a very large bank, with branches everywhere. In France, both Credit Agricole and Credit Lyonnais are very common banks. Some banks may require a mailable address in Europe, so be prepared. You may need a friend or a business to provide a permanent address.

Credit cards are as much in vogue in Europe as in the US. MasterCard prevails in Holland, while VISA is dominant in France. Elsewhere both are generally accepted. American Express is a distant third among American-also cards. (The EuroCard is quickly becoming very popular, but you don't need it.) The only advantage we found to American Express is its mail holding services at locations in Europe (see "Mail" below).

It is possible to draw a cash advance from some banks and currency exchange offices with a credit card, though be sure to check the fees in advance. In some cases, we found there were no fees (other than our local bank fee), and quite a good exchange rate.

MAIL

Those cruising for a month or less can ignore this section. Longer term cruisers, however, may get a yen to read what is happening back home.

Unfortunately, there is no simple solution to this one. There are two main alternatives, but both require one essential ingredient--a pre-planned itinerary. That may seem rather simple, but we found that part of the cruising joy was to find a spot we fell in love with, and to stay a few days for exploration and discovery. We had prepared an itinerary--and a re-vised itinerary--and a re-revised itinerary, until finally we gave up and said, *"Well, we think this fall we will probably be in France."*

Meanwhile, our friends dutifully had sent letters to the American Express offices according to "Schedule A", prepared well before our departure. When we failed to show until after the rather brief mail-holding time limit had expired, our mail was returned to sender, leaving us deeply disappointed and our friends mystified.

Were we to do it again, we would provide "short term schedules". We would write our friends that they could reply if they wrote immediately, and give them a city we planned to be in one month from the time we sent our letter to them. That would give sufficient time for our letter to arrive and them to respond. If we adjusted our schedule, as we inevitably did, we still would have a sufficient grace period to be sure the mail was not destroyed or returned to sender.

Have friends send letters (no packages, for security reasons) to the city post office addressed *"General Delivery--hold for personal pick up"*. The postal system will hold the letter a reasonable period of time. When you arrive, it is much easier to get directions in a strange town to the *"Post"*, than it is to the American Express office. And every town has a post office.

FAX

France has public FAXing at many of their Post Offices. Use it in combination with the money saving practices under telephone, below, and it is quite possible to communicate quickly and inexpensively. You can also receive FAXes if you will be in one town awhile.

E-MAIL

The art of E-mail at this writing remains just that for the cruising barger--an art more than a science. You need to have an acoustic coupler that fits European phones, unless you have a friend whose telephone jack you can use. Someday I am sure you will be able to get E-mail through the PCMCIA slot on your laptop, when connected with a cell or satellite phone. Check with a very knowledgeable computer guru before you depart for the latest in this rapidly changing field.

TELEPHONE

Don't leave home without the "card". Call your long distance carrier and ask them to send you a card that lists the international access codes that enable you to reach them from a foreign country.

Why? Because it is **much** cheaper. All US telephone companies are much more reasonable than their European counterparts. (If you don't know already, **never** telephone internationally from a hotel room except to call your US long distance carrier, which is a toll-free call. It is common for hotels to double or triple telephone charges as a "service charge". The same is true for laundry.) The card from your long distance carrier will list foreign countries alphabetically, with a telephone access number beside each country. To place a toll-free call to your US long distance carrier, go to any public telephone in the European country you happen to be in at the moment, get the dial tone, call up your US carrier and they will place the call for you. During our stay, the time of day we placed the call did not matter--the rate was the same: about $1 a minute, plus a per call setup charge of several dollars.

Recently a telephone credit carrier called Premiere World Link (1-800-432-6169) established less expensive calls from Europe to the US. They have two rates: one for direct calls from Europe, and another--less than half the price--whereby you call their toll-free number, hit *9, dial in the phone number you are calling from, and hang up. The computer calls you back and you then place the call to the US number. Calls are billed to your standard credit card.

Investigate and arrange your calling scheme before you go, depending upon the best deal at the time of your departure in this highly competitive and volatile marketplace.

Although there is no charge to call your US carrier using the access code, some European telephones require that you deposit money in the telephone before using it. You get it back after the call. And therein can lie a little challenge.

European telephone companies are gradually transitioning from coin telephones to card telephones. On these new fangled phones, instead of inserting a coin, there is a credit card type slot at the top where one inserts a special telephone calling card. The telephone card, which may be purchased at the post office, has a number of prepaid "units" which are electronically calculated by a computer inside each telephone. The computer makes an invisible imprint on the calling card, subtracting units depending on the distance and length of the call.

The advantages to the European telephone company are two-fold: labor savings in not having to collect the coins from thousands of public telephones, and avoiding "cash" theft problems. Interestingly, some cards had special designs which made them collectors' items. The telephone "swallowed" the card automatically when it was fully expended and collectors sometimes broke into the telephone to get the used up cards, strictly for their collector value.

The advantage of the cards to the consumer is convenience and cost savings. It is cheaper to call by card than by coin; and, one does not need an array of coins ready for constant feeding.

The disadvantage for us cruisers is that we seldom use the card for anything other than the toll-free international access call. Buy the cheapest card, generally $5 to $10. Newer phones require no card for access.

The only additional inconvenience is that during the transition from coin to card phones, there are both. And of course one cannot use coins in a card phone, nor cards in a coin phone. So before setting off in search of a phone booth, grab a coin as well as the local phone card before you leave the barge.

Other than the card/coin confusion, I found the European public telephone system wonderfully simple to use. First, they are easy to spot. Phone booths are always the same color in a given country (except, of course, France): green in Holland, red in Britain, yellow in Germany. France had "variety". But the best part is the little screen on the telephone that shows what number you have dialed, how much money you have inserted (in case of a coin phone) plus the balance left (or how many calling "units" are left on your phone card). The one thing the little screen cannot tell you, of course, is the amount of the bill adding up at your US carrier for that call back to the States.

We discovered before we left for Europe that our USAA (United Services Automobile Association, available to past and present US Armed Services members) Gold MasterCard entitled us to use a message service, at no charge. We could place a collect call from anywhere in the world and check for messages from friends or business associates. In the US, the message could be placed by telephoning an 800 number. Although there were limits on the length of the message and the number of times it could be called in a month, we used this service extensively. It gave us peace of mind that all was well on the home front. If a business or personal problem back home arose, our friends left a message for us to call them. It worked wonderfully.

I do not know how many banks contract for this message service as part of their credit card "deal", but it may be worth checking.

In lieu of the message service, we recommend that you set a schedule to call a particular key person at home. Let your associates know that they can leave messages for you by contacting that person. Then call once a week or so, using the access code for your US long distance carrier.

After a few months cruising in a foreign country, it feels good just to hear the operator answer with that good ole accent from home!

CRUISING CAMARADERIE

One also feels strangely warm toward one's native tongue and countrymen after months abroad. The Stars and Stripes flying from the stern brought toots, hollers, waves, and instant camaraderie as complete strangers suddenly felt like long lost neighbors, though we'd never met before.

It was also wonderful to hear the charming British accent emerge from among the foreign tongues. We discovered in our own way why the "special relationship" exists. The British have taken to barging in a big way. The Dutch Barge Association, a British club, provides excellent counsel and camaraderie for English speaking canaliers, as well as a highly readable newsletter for an annual membership fee of about $50. Address: Burleigh House, Attn: Balliol Fowden
273 Hillmorton Road, Rugby, England CV22-5BH
FAX 011-44-1788-891-934

Chapter 10

HOW TO BUY THE RIGHT BARGE

The dream won't let go. You must do this cruise. You want to purchase your own floating European home. Here are some guidelines from our experience that you may find helpful.

WHERE TO BUY

Holland is the best place to buy, France the best place to sell. The Netherlands simply has so many boats to choose from that it is much more a buyer's market than most other countries. Plus, with a wide variety of shapes and sizes, conditions, and degrees of finish, you are much more likely to find a barge that fits both your preferences and your budget.

If however, you are specifically looking for a retired "peniche" and you have the time and patience, the best peniche bargains are to be found in Belgium. These are basic black freight barges and require substantial investment to convert to livable and cruisable condition. Because they squeeze into locks with just inches to spare, even when equipped with a bowthruster, they require skill and experience to cruise. No single-handling here! Because of their sheer size, these are the vessels of choice for conversion to the "luxury cruise" barges on the French waterways. Not much for exterior style, but the interior can be made to suit the exquisite tastes of the designer with a checkbook.

For most cruisers, however, the choice is Holland for barge shopping. Sources for finding barges are two: from private parties and through brokers. Private listings may be found in local newspapers, but primarily in the large city newspapers, especially Amsterdam.

We tried newspapers without much success. It was difficult to get a good description over the phone, and then we had to locate each potential "find", usually in one of Holland's innumerable obscure moorings.

The other source is brokers. Dutch brokers operate differently than American brokers. In the US, a "multiple listing" network enables one to shop for a knowledgeable broker. The broker then, in addition to checking his or her own listings, searches the nation, region, or world, for a selection of boats listed by other brokers that meets the customer's criteria. The listing and selling brokers share the 10% sales commission (paid by the seller), 7% to the selling broker and 3% to the listing broker.

From a buyer's viewpoint, this system has the advantage of letting the professional broker find the best boat at the best price, saving the customer a lot of time and work.

In Holland, on the other hand, the commission is normally 8% and fewer brokers are willing to share that commission in a multiple listing arrangement. As a result, instead of shopping for a reputable and responsive broker, the buyer frequently must scour the listings personally. Some individuals, chiefly surveyors, will make the search for a fee, generally 10% over the selling price.

To my knowledge, only one US brokerage, San Juan Sailing (which I own) #1 Harbor Esplanade, Bellingham, Washington 98225 (360-671-4300, FAX 360-671-4301, E-mail: Sailsjs@aol.com) offers a no-charge barge finding service in Europe.

Some Dutch brokers share advertising costs by jointly publishing magazines with photos and brief descriptions of their boats. Other brokers have networks that operate under the same name, and also publish magazines which highlight their listings.

We found three primary such magazines: one by the world's largest brokerage, Vander Valk; a second by the multiple brokerage firm called *"Het Wakend Oog"* (the observant eye), published by European Yachtbrokers, c/o Yachtbrokerage *"Het Wakend Oog"* b.v., P.O. Box 70 8530 AB Lemmer, The Netherlands); and a cooperative venture listing magazine of about twenty brokers called *"Jacht & Bootgids"* (published by De Haan and Broese, Postbus 1, 8625 ZK Oppenhuizen, Friesland, The Netherlands, FAX 011-31-51-555-9382). I consider De Haan the premier barge broker. The magazines have sections for powerboats, sailboats, *"Platbodems"* (flat bottoms), and *"Ex-Beroepsvaartuigen"* in some of the magazines, which refers more specifically to barges without sails. You want to look for barges in this last section, or, if there is no such section, they will have included barges with *Platbodems*.

The *Platbodems* include beautiful new or nearly new sailing varieties like *Skutjes*, ornate replicas of the sturdy traditional craft that, with lee-boards on either side, plied the shallow lakes and bays of the Netherlands for centuries. Though fine works of craftsmanship--and as a sailor I find this painful to admit--these sailing craft are not suitable for the rugged demands of the inevitable bump and grind of countless locks and docks.

Visiting various brokerages is an educational experience, and sooner or later, you will find the best boat for your purposes. Fortunately, Holland is a small country, and even the remotest brokerages are but a few hours apart via the speedy freeways, cutting down considerably on shopping time.

An enterprising Dutch firm, Inter-Ocean, has ventured into computerized sales listings with brokers willing to share commissions. They also provide a succinct guide to barge selection which you may download from their internet site. Inter-Ocean Shiplease, PO Box 6486, 1005 EL Amsterdam, The Netherlands. 011-31-20-620-6646; FAX 011-31-20-625-8555; E-mail: interocean@dataplace.nl.

In our barge buying experience, we allocated two weeks for the barge selection process and were ready for the "family vote" after 10 days of intensive boat shopping.

We also used our shopping experience as an opportunity to ask questions of whomever we encountered--prospective surveyors, brokers, boaters, and chandlers. Some of the best advice came from Dik de Haan, a surveyor: "*Forget a fancy boat. Get a practical one. Make sure she is solid, with a good engine, and plenty of ballast.*"

Dik de Haan, Postbus 14, 5317 ZG Nederhemert, The Netherlands, FAX 011-31-418-55-2858.

I reflected on those words both during our selection and during our journey, appreciating his wisdom more each kilometer.

BALLAST

Ballast is one of the most important criteria in boat selection. Check the listing sheet for total weight and ballast. Then put them in a ratio.

For a steel barge, it is desirable that ballast equal 50% of the total weight (the ballast weighs the same as the barge sans ballast). The amount of ballast will aid in directional control, and keep the barge cooler in summer and warmer in winter.

If the barge is lightly ballasted, determine how easy it would be to add ballast, either by poured concrete, pieces of metal, or additional tankage. (See additional discussion in Chapter 3). If the barge is unballasted, and balanced ballast is difficult, shop for a different one, unless you plan to heavily insulate the vessel and to install a powerful bowthruster, or plan to cruise only in the cooler climes and larger locks of Holland and Belgium.

As we visited with fellow bargers during our extended cruise, the single greatest recurring complaint concerned lack of ballast, especially among those cruising in France.

France has two features about its cruising which make ballast important. First, the locks are narrow (Napoleonic) and are a challenge to enter under the best of circumstances. A lightly ballasted barge, with her flat bottom, exposed superstructure, and almost no underwater portion to resist sideways force, is highly susceptible to side winds, making entry into the locks difficult and at times very frustrating.

The second complaint in France is that, with her warmer climate, the barge can become uncomfortably hot. The sun can be unmerciful on a steel hull. A properly ballasted barge has less metal exposed to the sun, more immersed in cooler water. So it not only handles better, but the temperature is more comfortable as well.

Ballasting can be accomplished in several ways: poured concrete, metal pieces, and tankage. Poured concrete and tankage are most common. Metal pieces are normally used only for spot ballasting, or balancing of the ballast. In our barge, for example, the previous owner thought the barge sat a bit bow heavy, so he added chunks of cast iron below the bunks in the aft cabin.

Another barging acquaintance, Nick de Vries, who did his own conversion from cargo to liveaboard, used only tankage for ballast. Of course, to be useful, the tanks need to be full, so plan carefully. Water ballast is the most common, although having substantial reserves for diesel can be very useful if you fuel up in Belgium for a year of cruising in France.

Calculate how high in the water the barge will be when the tanks are nearly empty to make sure the barge can still clear the lowest of the fixed bridges along the route!

The quality of fuel is also important, since all fuels deteriorate after time and poorer fuels have a relatively brief shelf life. Inquire with local commercial bargers for the best evaluation of local fuels.

Flexible tanks are preferred. The most common are made by den Ouden Vetus of Holland. Being constructed of synthetics, these tanks don't rust, are much easier to install, fit the contours of their placement area, and, perhaps most importantly, don't cause condensation when partially full, in contrast to metal tanks. Proper placement for balanced ballast is important, both when the tanks are full, and when water and fuel are drawn down, so you don't end up listing to either port or starboard.

Since the advent of the Vetus type tanks, tankage ballast seems to have replaced poured concrete as the ballast of choice on recent liveaboard conversions. On earlier conversions, however, poured concrete will be the most common.

It is very important to assure that poured concrete ballast has been accomplished properly. If the seal between the hull and the concrete is improper, condensation and air continually feed rusty spots. Worse, repairing the rusty spot is virtually impossible without chipping out the concrete. How to check for problems? First, find out which yard poured the concrete. A knowledgeable surveyor will know the reputation of the yard, even if the work was done 50 years ago. Second, have the surveyor check hull thickness (discussed in more detail later in this chapter). If the hull is thin around the turn of the bilge, it may indicate a problem. Given the age of these vessels, however, if the hull wears thin every 50 years or so, so what? Steel plates can be welded over any thin spots at relatively modest cost. If, on the other hand, plates have been welded on, *and*, they have worn thin, it bears further investigation. There may be a continuing problem.

BOWTHRUSTERS

Let me restate a theme throughout this book: if a barge lacks proper ballasting, bowthrusters may well be needed. Given a choice between a barge with proper ballast or a barge with a bowthruster, I will choose the properly ballasted barge. Indeed, a bowthruster on a listing for sale may indicate an added convenience, or it may indicate improper ballasting. Immediately check the ballast to weight ratio.

For a more detailed discussion of bowthrusters, see Chapter 3, *Stopping and Turning*.

ENGINE

I wish there were a sure-fire way to evaluate with absolute certainty the condition of an engine. After all, it is the heart of the barge and its health and your happiness are closely intertwined.

Unless the surveyor is specifically qualified in engine analysis, the condition of the motor is usually excluded from the scope of the survey. So, either you or another expert will need to be employed to analyze the engine. Get an expert whose judgment you trust. Go to a local chandlery, a commercial barge yard, and an automotive service manager (all three). Ask each of them to recommend the most knowledgeable barge diesel engine mechanic they know. When you hear the same name come up at least twice, you've got your person. Engage them to test your engine.

There is always some element of risk with any engine. These are a few items to check that can reduce the degree of risk.

1. **Reputable brands**. Having a proven, popular model both reduces the chance of problems and assures better availability of reasonably priced parts. Brands like Mercedes and DAF (Dutch made diesel) are solid. There will be some Ford Lehmans. The occasional Caterpillar is top of the line, but other than that, I would be very careful of purchasing a barge with an off brand. Check with the best mechanic locally about the frequency of repairs and the cost of parts for the engine you are examining.

Rebuilt engines, especially when rebuilt by the factory, can be nearly as good as new, and usually have a warranty. The DAF 575, about 100 horsepower (horsepower, or PK in Holland, is measured and reported in different ways) is a reliable, very common engine for barges.

2. **Engine hours**. The fewer the engine hours, the longer the life left, at least in theory, depending upon how it was maintained and the type of use it had. Operating at a constant medium RPM is the best use. Lots of stops and starts is the worst. Operating with too large a propeller, too small a propeller, or an improperly sized transmission can also be harmful.

3. **Engine history**. Beyond the type of work, try to get a maintenance history. Talk to the person who did the maintenance. A history of frequent repairs probably means a future of frequent repairs.

4. **Engine test**. With the permission of the seller, run a simple engine test, that, according to Arend Bonsink., our master mechanic, is the best way to test the condition of an engine. Tie the barge securely to a stout dock. Idle the engine five minutes to warm it up. Then engage the transmission, running it at medium RPM until it comes to temperature. Note the operating temperature for reference. Then move it to 3/4 of maximum RPM for ten minutes. Finally, run it at maximum throttle for 15 minutes. Monitor oil pressure and engine temperature throughout the test.

Arend Bonsink and a brother own Aquaservice, Westeinde 6, 8064 AK Zwartsluis, NL FAX 011-31-38 3866005. Between Arend and his several brothers, I doubt there is anything regarding boats they cannot do—and do very well.

Watch for smoke from the exhaust. Some smoke initially means it is burning out accumulated carbon. Once up to maximum speed, however, the degree of smoke indicates how much oil is being burned, and consequently, the compression and condition of the cylinders and valves. Black smoke indicates problems--incomplete combustion or burning oil.

Running the engine at these RPMs, Arend reports, will put all engine system components to the test and show any weaknesses.

Always have someone near the engine controls to immediately shut down if there are big problems, like a sudden rise in temperature. A radiator hose may break, a belt may give way, the fuel filter may partially clog--all indicators of potential problems.

5. **Compression check**. If the engine run shows significant black smoke at maximum rpm, a compression check can help show whether this is due to worn rings and cylinders, or valve problems.

6. **Oil analysis**. Although this requires both expert extraction (the right temperature, the right amount of time after oil change) and interpretation,

this controversial analysis can sometimes help indicate the source of problems.

There are many facets to engine condition, and I do not begin to cover all of them here. The best counsel I have received is to do test #4 above. It costs nothing but some fuel, and, assuming the seller's consent (especially should something break on the engine), is the best and cheapest engine analysis available.

SURVEY

A competent professional survey is one of the buyer's best tools. As a person professionally involved with sailboats (charters, sailing school, sales), I would never make a sale without recommending a survey. The critical choice a buyer must make is who to employ as surveyor. Competence varies widely and a buyer should be wary of anyone recommended by a dealer or salesperson. There are too many buddy-buddy relationships. The surveyor should be working for the benefit of the buyer, not that of the dealer or salesperson.

Start with the largest local marine insurance agency. Ask them for two or three recommendations. There also may be other sources for recommendations.

In Holland, there is a national association of marine surveyors. I contacted the president and asked if he was available. When he was not, I asked his recommendation. Unfortunately, his recommendation turned out to be a poor one. The old gent spent most of his 20 minutes aboard the vessel taking notes from the seller, cast a glance here and there, gave the underbody a few bangs with his hammer and left. A few days later I received a report in Dutch (the surveyor spoke no English) and a bill for $500 (the buyer pays for the survey), which I figured was a bit high for the cursory tour he made of the vessel. He didn't test any systems or equipment and didn't measure the thickness of the hull. The survey (after translation) covered nothing I did not already know and did not address a lot I did know--things that were wrong with the boat that I subsequently had to repair or replace. All of which goes to show that there are no guarantees of solid surveyorship. I should have checked this person out with more sources. When I shared my disappointment with the broker, he just smiled, shrugged, and said, *"Well, he was the one you wanted."*

Definitely be present for the survey and insist the surveyor check at least these items:

- thickness of the hull.
- areas of deck rusting.
- drive train condition and lubrication, and propeller. He should comment on the propeller size and type for the weight and draft of the vessel.
- steering system.
- electrical system: condition, capacity, rates of discharge and recharge.
- plumbing systems.
- condition of heads.
- heating system.
- some comment on engine size, brand, and condition.
- condition of onboard equipment.
- suitability for the region you will be cruising, and for the type of cruising you will be doing.
- amount and condition of ballasting material.
- recommendation for improvements and repairs, prioritized.

No boat is perfect. After all, she's only human! Every survey will find something wrong. Or should. If the surveyor finds no fault, either the surveyor is incompetent or the boat is so perfect you cannot afford it.

If the fault list is short, be thankful. If there are significant deficiencies, or major repairs (the batteries are shot, the propeller has a hairline crack at a blade root, the grease gun is too small to service the shaft packing gland), you have grounds to negotiate some price reduction. Don't be a nitpicker, but if there are substantial defects, some consideration is in order.

AGE

Generally, older is better. Personally, I wouldn't even look at a barge younger than I am. Who wants a new, untested vessel? Or even a young 50 year old model? Now, if she was built around the turn of the century, she's had time to prove herself. Really!

Generally, prior to 1900 hulls were constructed of iron. Contrary to what one might think, iron hulls rust less than steel. These 19th century boats make the best hulls.

Barges constructed from 1900-1915 are made of steel, and generally good steel. This was the heyday of barge construction. Barges, other than peniches and the modern huge variety, are an oddity if built other than between 1880 to 1915.

For more on hulls and rusting, see Chapter 8, *Equipment*.

INSULATION

It's a good idea. The more the better. As you can imagine, living in a steel box can get quite uncomfortable on a hot summer day. Conversely, nothing seems quite as chilly as cold steel in the snow.

The big challenge with insulating steel is to avoid condensation. If air gets between the steel and the insulation, droplets will form, promoting rust and destroying the insulating properties of the material.

Our hull was insulated in what I considered an innovative way. Fiberglass insulation was stuffed into plastic tubes which were exactly the width of the ship's hull ribs. The plastic tubes were then sealed with tape and laid between the steel ribs. The plastic prevented any condensation from getting at the insulation. Overhead, sheets of foam insulation were affixed.

Andre du Pont, a French friend of mine inherited huge problems with his new British built barge because the insulation was secured to the overhead and walls by screws into the steel deck and superstructure. Of course, the screws were as cold as the exterior steel. When their heads were exposed to the warm moist air inside the barge, the screws acted like hundreds of tiny dripping faucets. The resulting condensation degraded his insulation, corroded his wiring, and made his living room a rain forest.

Fortunately for the boat buyer, rusty drippings leave tell tales that are easy to spot. Be sure to look carefully for them, especially in corners and edges where a fresh coat of paint may not have covered the evidence.

BARGE TYPES

The date of construction and the region where they were built will determine the style of barge. Barges back then were far from the rectangular boxes of black steel that we Americans think of when we hear the word "barge". Back then, they were a stylish art form, skillfully designed, meticulously constructed, and lovingly maintained. The appearance of one's barge made a statement about the owner--their style, professionalism, and standards of cleanliness. The barges were anything but drab black. They were dressed in bright colors and bedecked with fresh flowers. Each region of the small country developed its unique style of barge construction that the old timers still instantly recognize.

Functionally, there is little difference between the various styles (at least to you and I). It's rather like buying a car. The style should be esthetically pleasing to you. After all, your barge is a lady, and she should be loved.

How Big a Barge?

How big a barge to buy? That question has a different answer for each person. Part of the answer will be budget and part will be the amount of room needed. The other practical factor in the equation is that the larger the barge, the more difficult she can be to handle.

If you plan to travel to France or Belgium, make sure she can fit in the Napoleonic locks (barge no larger than 38.5 meters long by 5 meters wide). The greater the beam, the less room to spare when entering the French locks. Skill is a factor, but in our experience you get to be as good as you need to be. After all, the "peniches", with a crew of two (total!) squeeze themselves with only inches of clearance.

Height is also a factor. Bridges are generally the lifting type in Holland and height is not a problem there. France, on the other hand, has a fixed bridge at virtually each lock (and thousands of locks). If you plan to cruise in France, make sure the superstructure height above water is no more than 3.1 meters, which is suitable for the fixed bridges on most canals, or 2.7 meters, the maximum on some sections of the Nivernais Canal. Many barges have removable pilothouses for the exceptional low bridge. Check ease of removal and, based on your intended cruising area, how often you will need to break it down.

On larger Dutch canals, draft is no problem. On smaller Dutch canals, or on French canals, a draft of 1.4 meters will get you through most canals, a draft of 1.2 meters means no problem on virtually any canal.

My ideal barge would be about 20 meters long (shorter if there were just two of us), 4 meters wide, with a 1 meter draft and a maximum height above water of 2.7 meters. Large enough to be comfortable and capable of going on virtually any canal on the Continent, especially the quaint smaller ones.

TAXES

The tax in Europe that will affect you is the VAT, or Value Added Tax. In Holland it is called the *BTW* (pronounced "Bay Tay Vay"). The rate is high, generally 17.5% to 20%. Unlike the sales tax, the VAT is only collected once during the lifetime of a particular item—at its point of original retail sale. It can be resold many times thereafter, but once the VAT has been paid, it need not be paid again. Consequently, there is no VAT on used boats, only on new ones.

Because the tax is only collected at the point of original retail sale, all components purchased to bring the item to the point of retail sale are tax exempt. For example, because the VAT on a new boat is collected at the time it is sold to the first retail buyer all purchases by the boat builder for the equipment and components used to construct the boat, such as the engine, rudder, and steering wheel, are exempt from the VAT (though technically "exempt" is not the right term, the effect is the same because the manufacturers and wholesalers pay the VAT and then get credit for it for resale). This VAT exemption is not relevant to the barge buyer. But there are two important exemptions that do apply.

If you purchase a significant amount of equipment, it may be helpful to know that goods destined for export are exempt from the VAT. A purchase within a particular country for resale *or use* within another country is exempt. The idea is that the person importing the item will be assessed a tax by the country into which it is imported. One aid to help qualify for a tax exemption on equipment for your barge is to register the barge with the American Consulate in the country in which it is purchased. Because a boat registered to an American owner is considered an American boat, the new American owner is entitled to fly the American flag. Showing your American registration makes it easier to avoid the VAT when making purchases for your barge.

The second exemption applies if the barge is placed in charter. This is more complicated, however, because then you must form a company in the country where the charter is located, collect the VAT on all charter fees, and of course be subject to all the regulations of the host country for your type of business. It is always more difficult for a foreigner owning a local business than for a local national owning the business. My advice is that unless particularly unusual circumstances warrant, do not set up a local business in order to qualify for a VAT exemption on supplies purchased.

If you plan to conduct charters, establish an American business and operate the barge as your own in Europe. But that subject is beyond the scope of this book..

Some businesses in Holland who sell regularly to foreigners for export (like chandleries close to a border) get a special permit from their government that allows them to submit exempted sales en masse, keeping a record of the foreigner's name and address for audit purposes. These businesses are by far the simplest to buy tax exempt from. We found the Koos Slurink Chandlery in Zwartsluis, NL to be most helpful. They are well-stocked, honest, and speak English fluently.

The process to reclaim VAT after a purchase from other "normal" businesses is more complicated. First, there is a minimum purchase amount set by the government (usually about $100) to qualify for a refund. Second, the buyer must first pay the tax, then get the receipt stamped by local customs officials as he leaves the country with the goods. Then he must mail the stamped receipt to the store where he made the purchase. The store will then reimburse the buyer for the VAT. If he has a bank account in their country, or if he made the purchase on credit card, the refund process is much easier. For a barge owner, this procedure requires receipts and the addresses for each tax exemptible purchase. He must find the national customs agent (Dutch *Douane* if the purchase was in Holland) at the waterway border as the barge departs the country, and persuade him or her to stamp it. The agent may refer the buyer to a border brokerage house to have the proper form filled out. Be sure to shop various brokerage houses to compare rates before engaging them.

If the customs agent wants to get technical, he may refuse to stamp the receipts because, though you are leaving the country with the goods, you have no evidence you are taking the purchased items to the country of export (in this case, the USA).

The process is hazy at best. If you have made thousands of dollars in purchases for your barge, the process is worth the chance you may get a substantial percentage back. Ask for tax exemptions. Take any that you can get. Don't worry about the rest. Other than buying from a chandlery that normally sells tax exempt for export, save yourself the hassle over small items. I consider the tax a tip for being able to use the locks and canals for such a bargain. And remember also, unlike in the US, you did not have to pay sales tax when you bought your barge!

FINANCING

If you plan to finance the barge purchase, arrange the financing back in the US. Banks are highly unlikely to use a barge in a foreign country as collateral, so you will need separate security for a loan. European banks are even more unlikely to loan money to foreigners, especially foreigners whose only collateral in the country is a highly mobile floating asset. It's best to have your financial arrangements made before you go barge shopping.

Inter-Ocean, referred to on page 144, also arranges de facto financing through an inventive "lease" program. Financing rates are likely to be more attractive back in the States, but Inter-Ocean may be an option to investigate.

FINAL NOTE

Boat buying practices in Europe are very similar to the US, with one exception. The European broker assumes that the buyer has received approval from the bank before taking the broker's time to look at boats. In the US, the bank is often the last stop.

The listing price is the hoped for price. Some sellers will hold to it, some will negotiate after receiving an offer. As a general rule, it is not unusual to submit an initial offer about 10% below the asking price. Of course, if you feel the barge is overvalued, offer a little less than you think it is worth, so the final agreed upon price is a fair one. Always make the offer subject to survey, engine test, and test cruise.

This final step is the big step. Become a barge owner, and you enter an entirely new lifestyle. It is almost like assuming a new identity. Only you can decide if you want to do it. My only advice is this: if you want to, do it. It took us seven years to arrange everything so we could "do it". If you are at all like us, the experience will transcend monetary value. Your barge will cruise into your heart, where it will go on cruising forever.

The crew of the *"Vertrouwen"* on our seventeen month family cruise about to explore Utrecht. From left: Danny, Justin, Minti, Jonathan, Marlene. We wore the treads off the tires.

EPILOGUE

We have returned to the "normal" American lifestyle as I edit the manuscript. With one shining exception. Shortly before our return from Europe, a few of my friends expressed interest in becoming partners in the barge when we completed our cruise. The idea spread like wildfire. We would not have to leave our beloved *"Vertrouwen"* forever, after all. We now have ten wonderful partners--friends--with whom we share glorious hours visiting and revisiting favorite cruising grounds. When the partners are not cruising, *"Vertrouwen"* is available for charter.

Instead of closing that chapter of my life, I have been able to delightfully re-open the book each year, either with family, friends, or charter guests.

As I reread these pages, the faces, feelings, and experiences of that extended family cruise flood over me. I realize we did not make the cruise as much as the cruise made us. It changed us permanently. Individually and as a family, we are broadened, deepened, and enriched. Although our cruise lasted but 17 months, it really has never ended. Our gentle wakes will lap against the grassy canal banks as long as memory lasts.

The author and his wife on the deck of *Vertrouwen*, moored in *Vertrouwen's* original 1908 homeport, the harbor of Zwartsluis.

Roger and Marlene Van Dyken and their children live in the small town of Lynden in the northwest corner of the United States. But for a year and a half they lived aboard their 1908 Dutch barge *Vertrouwen* with their children, ages eight to 20. They cruised over 3,000 miles and transited 915 locks as they explored the rivers and canals of Holland, Belgium, France, and Germany. For seven years they dreamed and planned for this "once in a lifetime" cruise. Then they gathered their children, boarded the plane, landed in Holland, and began the search for the "right barge". Thus began the great adventure that they now look back on as one of the most precious periods of their family life.

They expected it to end after 18 months. But *Vertrouwen* cruised permanently into their lives. Even though they have resumed "normal" life, they return regularly with friends and family to continue the traditions of the "great cruise". In fact, they added barge charters and sales to their sailboat firm's activities. Roger also hosts barge skipper training cruises.

Roger and Marlene own and operate San Juan Sailing in Bellingham, Washington, a sailing firm that provides sailboat charters in the San Juan Islands as well as sailing lessons and new and used sailboat sales. Both Roger and Marlene have been school teachers. Roger served three terms in the Washington State Legislature and is a colonel in the Air Force Intelligence reserve. Minti has subsequently served as an Army Intelligence Officer in the 82nd Airborne and is now married and enrolled in Johns Hopkins graduate program of Advanced International Studies. Justin attends Lubbock Christian University while Danny and Jonathan have rejoined their classmates at Lynden Christian Schools.

The author on the bank of France's River Doubs

Cedarbrook
131 East Cedar Drive
Lynden, WA 98264
(360)354-5770
FAX (360)671-4301